Voice of an Era

Voice of an Era

Mohammad Rafi's Golden Hits

Olivia K

Mohammed Altaf Hussain

CONTENTS

INDEX

Introduction

Music has the ability to captivate to rise above time, conveying with it the feelings, stories, and social subtleties of a period. In the dynamic embroidery of Indian film, hardly any voices have resounded as significantly as that of Mohammad Rafi. Brought into the world on December 24, 1924, in Kotla Ruler Singh, Punjab, Rafi's excursion from a little town to turning into the voice of ages is a demonstration of the extraordinary force of music.

The gathering collection named "Voice of a Period: Mohammad Rafi's Brilliant Hits" fills in as a gateway to return to and revel in the brilliant time of Hindi film. This contemplative excursion unfurls the layers of Rafi's imaginativeness, offering a nuanced comprehension of the man behind the voice and the permanent imprint he left on the Indian entertainment world.

The Man Behind the Voice

To comprehend the sorcery of Rafi's voice, one should dive into the conditions that formed the man himself. Brought up in a family with a profound love for music, Rafi's initial openness to different melodic impacts established the groundwork for his uncommon vocal reach. His inborn capacity to catch the spirit of an organization and implant it with feeling would proceed to characterize his heritage.From his modest starting points in the town to his introduction to playback singing, the account of Rafi's life is an account of diligence, energy, and a relentless obligation to his specialty. As he left on his melodic excursion, teaming up with nearby performers and gradually establishing himself, much to his dismay that his voice would reverberate through the passageways of time.

Exploring the Brilliant Period

The "Voice of a Period" gathering carefully organizes Rafi's brilliant hits, taking audience members on a nostalgic excursion through the realistic scene of post-freedom India. This was a time set apart by social renaissance, and Rafi's voice turned into the harbinger of progress, epitomizing the soul of a country tracking down its character.The early hits, enhanced with the effortlessness of structure and the wealth of verses, set up for Rafi's fleeting ascent. Tunes like "Tum Jo Mil Gaye Ho" and "Chaudhvin Ka Chand Ho" grandstand his vocal ability as well as his capacity to convey complex feelings with an easy appeal. The cooperation with music chiefs like Naushad and O.P. Nayyar during this period hardened Rafi's situation as the go-to playback artist for entertainers and authors the same.

Adaptability: The Rafi Range

One of the most striking aspects of Mohammad Rafi's imaginativeness is his unmatched adaptability. Whether it was the spirit blending ghazals, the enthusiastic and foot-tapping numbers, or the reflection songs, Rafi's voice flawlessly navigated across kinds. This part of the gathering is a festival of his chameleon-like capacity to adjust to the different melodic scene of Indian film.The melancholic kinds of "Yeh Duniya Yeh Mehfil" pull at the heartstrings, while the irresistible enthusiasm of "Aaja Principal Hoon Pyar Tera" welcomes audience members to move in celebration. The range of Rafi's collection isn't simply a demonstration of his vocal reach yet in addition a tribute to his obligation to serving the story of every melody.

Fitting with Maestros

A crucial part in Rafi's process is his joint effort with unbelievable music writers. The collection complicatedly winds around together the orchestra of Rafi's voice with the virtuoso of writers like S.D. Burman, Shankar-Jaikishan, and R.D. Burman. Every coordinated effort is a melodic exchange, a combination of two imaginative spirits uniting to make immortal tunes.S.D. Burman's structures, for example, "Chhod Do Aanchal" and "Yeh Jo Mohabbat Hai," mirror the deep class that characterized the period. In the interim, the vivacious rhythms of Shankar-Jaikishan's "Yahoo! Chahe Koi Mujhe Junglee Kahe" feature the extravagance and satisfaction that Rafi easily brought to his versions. The later joint efforts with R.D. Burman, found in tunes like "Mera Man Tera Pyasa" and "Chookar simple man ko," denoted a combination of conventional and contemporary sounds, preparing for the developing melodic scene.

A Sonic Narrative of Mid-twentieth Century India

The gathering catches the tunes as well as fills in as a sonic narrative of the socio-social milieu of mid-twentieth century India. Rafi's voice turned into the setting for a developing country, repeating the fantasies, goals, and sentiments of an age encountering the unavoidable trends.Melodies like "Zindagi Ke Safar Mein" epitomize the soul of flexibility and trust that characterized the post-freedom time. The heartfelt songs, for example, "Tere Simple Sapne Stomach muscle Ek Rang Hai," mirror the blooming of affection in a country tracking down its balance. Rafi's interpretations of enthusiastic tunes, as "Kar Chale Murmur Fida," reverberate with the intensity of a country commending its solidarity.

Getting through Heritage

As the collection advances, it becomes clear that "Voice of a Period" isn't simply a gathering however a demonstration of Rafi's getting through heritage. His voice, saved in these brilliant hits, keeps on rising above time, dazzling the hearts of audience members across ages.The getting through allure of Rafi's music lies in its capacity to bring out a bunch of feelings. Whether it's the tragic aggravation of partition in "Commotion Dhal Jaye" or the cheerful festival in "Aanewala Buddy Janewala Hai," Rafi's voice fills in as an immortal ally to the human experience. The gathering, consequently, isn't simply a nostalgic excursion however a living demonstration of the everlasting status of genuine craftsmanship.

Welcoming New Ages

"Voice of a Period: Mohammad Rafi's Brilliant Hits" is a melodic odyssey that rises above time, welcoming both prepared Rafi devotees and novices to submerge themselves in the rich embroidery of Indian film. It is a challenge to investigate the subtleties of a former period, to feel the throbbing heartbeat of a country through the voice of its maestro.As the last notes of "Jeene Ke Hain Chaar Racket" disappear, one is left with the acknowledgment that Rafi's voice isn't simply a remnant of the past however a no nonsense element that keeps on forming the melodic scene of India. The gathering, completely, remains as a demonstration of the getting through force of music, a medium through which the reverberations of a period resound through the passageways of time, it are genuinely undying to advise us that a few songs.

1. **Brief overview of Mohammad Rafi's significance in the Indian film industry**
   The Indian entertainment world, frequently alluded to as Bollywood, is an embroidery woven with the strings of music, feelings, and narrating. In this energetic scene, one name reverberations as the decades progressed, rising above the limits of existence - Mohammad Rafi. His importance in the Indian entertainment world isn't just that of a playback vocalist; it is an adventure of a craftsman whose voice turned into the heartbeat of a country, forming the actual pith of Indian film.

   Early Life and Melodic Odyssey

   To comprehend Rafi's importance, one should dig into the underlying foundations of his melodic excursion. Brought into the world on December 24, 1924, in Kotla Ruler Singh, Punjab, Rafi's initial openness to music inside a profoundly melodic family established the groundwork for his remarkable ability.

   From the heartfelt kinds of Qawwali at the nearby dargah to the old style subtleties learned under Ustad Bade Ghulam Ali Khan, Rafi's early stages were an orchestra of different impacts that molded the tone of his voice.His introduction to playback singing was not quick, but instead a continuous development. Rafi's process started with neighborhood exhibitions and radio stations, where his voice grabbed the eye of writers and music chiefs. His underlying coordinated efforts during the 1940s denoted the undeveloped phase of a vocation that would before long bloom into a melodic peculiarity.

   The Brilliant Time of Hindi Film

   Rafi's domination harmonized with what is frequently hailed as the "Brilliant

Time" of Hindi film, a period from the last part of the 1940s to the 1960s. This was an age portrayed by the development of artistic legends, famous stories, and, obviously, the immortal tunes that Rafi would deliver. His initial hits, for example, "Tera Khilona Toota Balak" and "Suhani Raat Dhal Chuki," set up for his celebrated lifetime.The 1950s saw the juncture of Rafi's voice with the creations of maestros like Naushad, Shankar-Jaikishan, and S.D. Burman. The heartfelt interpretation of "Man Tarpat Hari Darsan Ko Aaj" from the film Baiju Bawra and the abundant "Yippee! Chahe Koi Mujhe Junglee Kahe" from Junglee exhibited his adaptability. Rafi's voice flawlessly explored the range of feelings, turning into a characteristic piece of the characters on screen.

Flexibility Exemplified

One of Rafi's characterizing attributes was his unrivaled adaptability. He easily coasted between types, delivering each with an artfulness that was unrivaled. From the intensity of enthusiastic songs of praise like "Kar Chale Murmur Fida" to the delicate types of heartfelt numbers like "Chaudhvin Ka Chand Ho," Rafi's voice turned into the material on which the feelings of the story were painted.The 1960s denoted a peak in Rafi's vocation as he embraced the changing soundscape of Indian music. The approach of the "bend" and "rock and roll" impacts in Bollywood music was flawlessly integrated into Rafi's collection. Melodies like "Aaja Primary Hoon Pyar Tera" from Teesri Manzil and "O Simple Sona Re" from Teesri Manzil exhibited his capacity to adjust to developing melodic patterns while keeping up with the pith of his vocal mark.

Song in Each Mind-set

One can't examine Mohammad Rafi without recognizing his capacity to pass a horde of feelings on through his voice. His interpretations were not simply melodic notes; they were a close to home odyssey. In "Jo Wada Kiya Woh Nibhana Padega," the audience can nearly feel the heaviness of the commitment implanted in Rafi's voice. On the other hand, the bubbly "Simple Samne Wali Khidki Mein" from Padosan catches the fun loving blamelessness of a maturing sentiment.

His dominance over communicating despairing is maybe generally tangible in "Yeh Duniya Yeh Mehfil" from Heer Raanjha, where the sentiment in his voice reflects the preliminaries of life. Rafi's voice filled in as a channel for the audience to navigate the scenes of delight, distress, love, and wistfulness, making him the quintessential narrator through tune.

Coordinated efforts with Maestros

The enchantment of Rafi's voice was additionally improved by his coordinated efforts with the absolute most prominent music arrangers of the time. S.D. Burman, with his spirit blending pieces, tracked down a dream in Rafi. The ageless "Chhod Do Aanchal" and "Yeh Jo Mohabbat Hai" stand as unfading demonstrations of the cooperative energy between the maestro's tunes and Rafi's vocals.Shankar-Jaikishan's pieces, portrayed by their imaginative game plans, tracked down reverberation in Rafi's voice. Their organization yielded pearls like "Jeene Ke Hain Chaar Commotion" from the film Mujhe Jeene Do and "Jaan Pehchaan Ho" from Gumnaam, both exhibiting the cooperative virtuoso that characterized a period.

The 1970s saw the rise of R.D. Burman, and Rafi flawlessly adjusted to the changing melodic scene. Melodies like "Aaj Mausam Bada Beimaan Hai" and "Chookar simple man ko" represent the combination of customary and contemporary sounds, denoting another section in their melodic partnership.

The Sonic Account of a Time

Past the songs, Rafi's voice filled in as a sonic narrative of a time set apart by cultural changes, social movements, and the developing personality of post-freedom India. The 1960s, specifically, saw a flood in enthusiastic enthusiasm, and Rafi's versions of tunes like "Kar Chale Murmur Fida" became songs of praise of public pride.

Heartfelt numbers, a staple of Hindi film, were raised higher than ever with Rafi's interpretations. "Tere Simple Sapne Stomach muscle Ek Rang Hai" and "Chaudhvin Ka Chand Ho" epitomized the pith of affection, catching the creative mind of an age with their immortal allure.

The reflection kinds of "Madhuban Mein Radhika Nache Re" and "Mera Man Tera Pyasa" exhibited Rafi's capacity to bring out otherworldliness through his voice. His versions in this class were not simply melodic exhibitions; they were a profound excursion, resounding with the shared mindset of a profoundly strict and various country.

Inheritance and Interminability

As the 1980s unfurled, Rafi's wellbeing started to decline, and on July 31, 1980, the maestro bid goodbye to the human world. Notwithstanding, the heritage he left behind perseveres, deified in the endless songs that keep on reverberating through the passageways of time. Rafi's voice rises above ages, finding reverberation not just in that frame of mind of the people who survived the Brilliant Time yet in addition in the playlists of trendy audience members investigating the wealth of retro Bollywood music.

His effect isn't bound to the domains of film; it reaches out into the social texture of India. In each festival, each snapshot of satisfaction, and each profound excursion, there is a Rafi tune that gives the soundtrack. His voice has turned into an immortal friend, a wellspring of comfort, and an extension associating dissimilar minutes in the embroidery of life.

Mohammad Rafi's importance in the Indian entertainment world is definitely not a simple reference in that frame of mind of playback singing; a creation keeps on playing in the hearts of millions. His voice, a conductor for feelings, a narrator in tune, and an impression of a period, epitomizes the actual soul of

Bollywood's Brilliant Time. Rafi's inheritance isn't limited by the imperatives of time; it is an everlasting tune, fitting with the beat of Indian film and, likewise, the heartbeat of a country.

2. **Introduction to the compilation album "Voice of an Era: Mohammad Rafi's Golden Hits"**

Music, similar to a mystical string, winds through the texture of time, interfacing hearts and ages. In the immense orchestra of Indian film, one name reverberations as an immortal song - Mohammad Rafi. His voice, an agreeable mix of feeling and virtuosity, characterized a period and made a permanent imprint on the social scene. "Voice of a Period: Mohammad Rafi's Brilliant Hits" isn't only a collection; it's a journey into the profound excursion of an incredible playback vocalist whose reverberation rises above time.

Setting the Stage: Rafi's Ability in Playback Singing

Prior to digging into the complexities of the gathering collection, it is fundamental to grasp the extent of Mohammad Rafi's effect on Indian playback singing. Brought into the world on December 24, 1924, in Kotla Ruler Singh, Punjab, Rafi's excursion into the universe of music was a demonstration of crude ability meeting tenacious assurance.His capacity to easily navigate sorts, from soul-mixing ghazals to foot-tapping perky numbers, made him the quintessential playback artist of his time. Rafi was not just a performer; he was a narrator whose voice turned into the medium through which the feelings of characters on the cinema tracked down articulation.

His coordinated efforts with prestigious music arrangers like S.D. Burman, Shankar-Jaikishan, and R.D. Burman raised the true to life experience, giving crowds a sonic excursion that reverberated with the ethos of the Brilliant Time.

Revealing the Gathering: A Sonic Odyssey

"Voice of a Time: Mohammad Rafi's Brilliant Hits" isn't simply a combination of melodies; it is an organized compilation that exemplifies the actual substance of Rafi's famous lifetime. Each track is a brushstroke on the material of time, illustrating the realistic and melodic scene of mid-twentieth century India. The collection fills in as a demonstration of Rafi's flexible collection, displaying the different tints and shades of his voice.

The Nostalgic Preface: Reverberations from An earlier time

The excursion starts with a nostalgic introduction, beholding back to the early hits that established the underpinning of Rafi's famous lifetime. Tunes like "Tum Jo Mil Gaye Ho" and "Chaudhvin Ka Chand Ho" bring out a feeling of sentimentality, shipping audience members to a period where songs were made with straightforwardness, yet resounded with significant feelings. The joint effort with S.D. Burman and different maestros during this period denoted the beginning of a melodic upset, and the reverberations of these early stages wait all through the gathering.

Flexibility Released: A Melodic Range

As the collection unfurls, it reveals the immense range of Rafi's flexibility. From the profound versions of strong ditties like "Yeh Duniya Yeh Mehfil" to the irresistible enthusiasm of lively numbers like "Aaja Fundamental Hoon Pyar Tera," Rafi's voice turns into a chameleon, adjusting to each inclination and kind with artfulness. The arrangement features how Rafi flawlessly changed starting with one melodic territory then onto the next, making a permanent imprint in each.

Blending with Maestros: A Melodic Ensemble

A fundamental section of the collection is devoted to Rafi's joint efforts with unbelievable music arrangers. The ensemble of his voice orchestrates with the virtuoso of S.D. Burman, making immortal songs that rise above the limits of time. Shankar-Jaikishan's structures track down a profound reverberation in Rafi's versions, making a melodic orchestra that catches the ethos of the time.The later parts of the collection dig into the combination of conventional and contemporary sounds, organized by R.D. Burman. The cooperation among Rafi and R.D. Burman delivered tunes like "Mera Man Tera Pyasa" and "Chookar simple man ko," which denoted a conversion of two melodic forces to be reckoned with, making a hear-able encounter that mirrors the developing soundscape of Bollywood.

Sonic Narrative of a Period: Music as a Time Machine

"Voice of a Time" isn't simply a gathering; a sonic narrative of a period saw critical socio-social movements. Rafi's voice fills in as a time machine, shipping audience members to an age where the country was finding its character post-freedom. His devoted versions, for example, "Kar Chale Murmur Fida," became songs of praise that resounded with the soul of a country in the pains of progress.Heartfelt ditties, the heartbeat of Hindi film, track down a unique spot in the collection. Each affection mixed note, whether it's "Tere Simple Sapne Stomach muscle Ek Rang Hai" or "Chaudhvin Ka Chand Ho," epitomizes the immortal charm of sentiment, making the gathering a mother lode of feelings.

Getting through Imaginativeness: Rafi's Heritage

As the collection approaches its decision, it becomes obvious that "Voice of a Time" is definitely not a simple compilation; it's a demonstration of the persevering through imaginativeness of Mohammad Rafi. His voice, saved in these brilliant hits, challenges the imperatives of time, welcoming audience members to drench themselves in reality as we know it where tunes were sung as well as resided. The gathering remains as a tribute to Rafi's heritage, an inheritance that keeps on moving, excite, and reverberate with crowds across ages.

Welcoming the Audience on a Melodic Excursion

"Voice of a Time: Mohammad Rafi's Brilliant Hits" isn't simply a gathering collection; it is an encouragement to set out on a melodic excursion through the records of Indian film. It coaxes both prepared Rafi fans and trendy audience members to investigate the enchantment of a time where music was a backup as well as a hero in the narrating of movies. This gathering is a festival of a maestro whose voice rises above time, conveying with it the feelings, stories, and social subtleties of an age that will be for the rest of time carved in the records of melodic history.

Chapter 1

Early Hits and Nostalgic Journey

The excursion of Mohammad Rafi, the unbelievable playback vocalist of the Indian entertainment world, started as a vibrant preface in the tranquil town of Kotla Ruler Singh, Punjab. Brought into the world on December 24, 1924, Rafi's initial openness to the rich melodic customs of his family and environmental elements sowed the seeds of a colossal ability that would proceed to reclassify the scene of Hindi film.

In the early long periods of his profession, Rafi's voice was a rising crescendo, slowly earning respect through nearby exhibitions and radio stations. The reverberations of these early days resounded with the profound tunes that would later turn into the sign of his renowned lifetime. This part unfurls the story of Rafi's initial hits, giving a nostalgic excursion into the beginning of a voice that would become inseparable from the Brilliant Period of Indian film.

1. **The Melodic Embroidery of Rafi's Early stages**
   To comprehend the early hits of Mohammad Rafi is to drench oneself in the woven artwork of his early stages. Brought up in a family with a profound love for music, Rafi's openness to different melodic impacts assumed a significant part in molding his novel vocal style. From the spirit blending Qawwalis at the neighborhood dargah to the old style subtleties learned under the direction of Ustad Bade Ghulam Ali Khan, Rafi's melodic training was a melange of custom and development.His inborn capacity to assimilate and incorporate different melodic kinds prepared for the adaptability that would later characterize his oeuvre. These early impacts sharpened Rafi's vocal expertise as well as imparted in him a significant comprehension of the close to home profundity that music could convey.

2. **Neighborhood Exhibitions and Acknowledgment: The Beginning of a Star**
   Rafi's excursion from neighborhood exhibitions to public acknowledgment was a demonstration of his excellent ability. His deep versions during exhibitions

in Lahore grabbed the eye of the commended arranger Shyam Sundar, who, dazzled by Rafi's voice, asked him to move to Mumbai — the focal point of the Indian entertainment world.

The 1940s denoted Rafi's entrance into the universe of playback singing, a space overwhelmed by laid out voices. His underlying raids were set apart by coordinated efforts with less popular writers, steadily preparing for open doors with additional noticeable figures in the business. Melodies like "Tera Khilona Toota Balak" and "Yahan Badla Wafa Ka" from the mid 1940s exhibited Rafi's emotive profundity and vocal artfulness.

3. **The Coordinated effort with Naushad: Baiju Bawra and Then some**

The defining moment in Rafi's vocation accompanied his cooperation with the amazing author Naushad. The soundtrack of the film "Baiju Bawra" (1952) turned into an achievement, highlighting a portion of Rafi's initial pearls. The spirit blending "Man Tarpat Hari Darsan Ko Aaj" and the sincerely charged "O Duniya Ke Rakhwale" showed Rafi's capacity to convey significant feelings, procuring him praise and laying out a well established organization with Naushad.The outcome of "Baiju Bawra" denoted a change in perspective in Rafi's vocation direction. His voice became inseparable from the lead entertainers of the time, and his capacity to decipher the profound subtleties of a tune raised him to the echelons of playback singing. The excursion with Naushad went on with films like "Mela" (1948), "Amar" (1954), and "Mughal-e-Azam" (1960), each adding to the melodic tradition of Rafi's initial hits.

4. **The Extravagance of Shankar-Jaikishan's Pieces**

The 1950s saw a powerful change in Bollywood music, set apart by the development of new music chiefs exploring different avenues regarding imaginative sytheses. Shankar-Jaikishan, an impressive pair, perceived Rafi's capability to inject essentialness into their tunes. The joint effort brought about a variety of melodies that exhibited the richness and liveliness of Rafi's voice.Tunes like "Yippee! Chahe Koi Mujhe Junglee Kahe" from "Junglee" (1961) and "Ehsaan Tera Hoga Mujh Standard" from "Junglee" (1961) became songs of devotion of youth and sentiment, encapsulating the time. The irresistible enthusiasm of these structures denoted a takeoff from the customary, catapulting Rafi into the core of the melodic insurgency of the 1960s.

5. **O.P. Nayyar and the Lively Numbers**

Rafi's joint effort with O.P. Nayyar added an unmistakable flavor to his collection, described by enthusiastic and foot-tapping numbers. The soundtrack of "Naya Daur" (1957) included the vigorous "Yeh Desh Hai Go Jawano Ka," a tribute to the soul of another India. The science between Nayyar's vivacious pieces and Rafi's dynamic interpretation made these tunes enduring top picks. The early hits with O.P. Nayyar displayed Rafi's flexibility, demonstrating that his voice could consistently adjust to assorted melodic styles. The foot-tapping rhythms of "Aaiye Meherbaan" and the fun loving sentiment in "Aankhon Hello Aankhon Mein" exhibited Rafi's capacity to infuse life into creations that reverberated with the changing yearnings of post-autonomy India

.

6. **The Ghazal Maestro: Rafi's Visit into Ghazals**

   While Rafi was praised for his ability in enthusiastic and heartfelt numbers, his introduction to the domain of ghazals added one more aspect to his creativity. "Chaudhvin Ka Chand Ho" from the film "Chaudhvin Ka Chand" (1960) stays a commendable piece, displaying Rafi's capacity to convey profound feelings with nuance and artfulness. The ghazal kind permitted him to investigate the subtleties of song and verse, uncovering a gentler, reflective side of his vocal reach.

   Rafi and S.D. Burman: An Evergreen Association

   The cooperation between Mohammad Rafi and S.D. Burman is a part in the chronicles of Bollywood music that stands as a demonstration of their aggregate virtuoso. The early hits from films like "Pyaasa" (1957) and "Guide" (1965) exhibit the cooperative connection between the maestro arranger and the maestro entertainer. Melodies like "Racket Dhal Jaye" and "Tere Simple Sapne Stomach muscle Ek Rang Hai" catch the profound embodiment of Rafi's voice wedded with Burman's immortal creations.

7. **The Deification of Sentiment: Rafi's Versions in Heartfelt Numbers**

   No investigation of Rafi's initial hits would be finished without digging into his commitments to the class of heartfelt anthems. Tunes like "Chaudhvin Ka Chand Ho" and "Tere Simple Sapne Stomach muscle Ek Rang Hai" encapsulate the immortal charm of sentiment in Hindi film. Rafi's voice, absorbed feeling, turned into the timeless soundtrack to the blooming romantic tales portrayed on the cinema. These heartfelt anthems not just exhibited the profundity of Rafi's vocal reach yet additionally showed his capacity to convey the heap feelings related with adoration. His versions became songs of devotion for sweethearts, inspiring a feeling of wistfulness that keeps on dazzling crowds across ages.

8. **Influence on Indian Film: Rafi's Voice as a Social Impetus**

Rafi's initial hits assumed a critical part in molding the soundscape of Indian film during an extraordinary period. The 1950s and 1960s denoted a social renaissance, and Rafi's voice resounded with the goals, dreams, and battles of a recently free country. His tunes became songs of praise of trust, love, and strength, mirroring the ethos of a period going through significant changes.

The effect of Rafi's initial hits reached out past the bounds of film music. His voice turned into a social impetus, impacting design, language, and normal practices. Rafi's tunes were not recently heard; they were lived, celebrated, and turned into a vital piece of the shared mindset of a country tracking down its character.

The Melodic Introduction to a Celebrated Profession

The investigation of Mohammad Rafi's initial hits and nostalgic excursion is a melodic visit through the beginning of a voice that would proceed to turn into the spirit of Indian film. From the rural reverberations of Punjab to the lively roads of Mumbai, Rafi's process reflected the direction of a country on the cusp of progress.The early hits structure the underpinning of Rafi's celebrated profession, every melody a demonstration of his developing masterfulness. The joint efforts with Naushad, Shankar-Jaikishan, O.P. Nayyar, and S.D. Burman displayed the flexibility of his voice, laying out him as the voice of an age. Whether in the rich rhythms of "Hurray! Chahe Koi Mujhe Junglee Kahe" or the spirit blending profundities of "Chaudhvin Ka Chand Ho," Rafi's initial hits stay scratched in the chronicles of melodic history, a persevering through demonstration of the wizardry of his voice.As the drape ascends on this nostalgic excursion, it abandons a melodic preface that makes way for the crescendo of Rafi's distinguished lifetime. The reverberations of these early hits wait, welcoming audience members to cross the immortal tunes that keep on resounding, rising above the limits of reality.

1.1 Exploration of Rafi's early career highlights

In the rural embroidery of Punjab, in the midst of the resonant reverberations of people tunes and the spirit mixing types of Qawwali, Mohammad Rafi made his most memorable strides towards a predetermination that would see him become the voice of an age. The early profession of Rafi was a melodious odyssey, an excursion from the peaceful scenes of his town to the clamoring roads of Mumbai, where his voice would reverberate through the hallways of Indian film.This investigation digs into the early stages of Rafi's profession, following the early features that molded the direction of a playback singing maestro. From nearby exhibitions to coordinated efforts with incredible writers, this section unfurls the parts of Rafi's melodic apprenticeship, establishing the groundwork for a vocation that would rethink the scene of Hindi film music.

1. **Melodic Impacts in Punjab: Sustaining a Wonder**

   Rafi's process started in Kotla Ruler Singh, a curious town in Punjab. Settled inside a family profoundly submerged in melodic customs, Rafi's openness to different classes of music was supported since the beginning. The town, with its dynamic social milieu, turned into the favorable place for the youthful wonder's melodic sensibilities.

   The impact of the nearby Qawwali customs, combined with the old style subtleties conferred by Ustad Bade Ghulam Ali Khan, made a remarkable melodic speculative chemistry in Rafi's initial preparation. His capacity to consistently mix people, old style, and reflection components laid the foundation for the flexible craftsman he would later turn into.

2. **The Excursion to Mumbai: An Act of pure trust**

   Rafi's relocation to Mumbai denoted the first huge achievement in quite a while profession. The clamoring city, with its colorful mix of societies and goals, gave the material on which Rafi would paint his melodic inheritance. The underlying years were a time of battle, as Rafi looked for open doors to exhibit his ability in the cutthroat domain of playback singing.The defining moment came when the famous writer Shyam Sundar perceived Rafi's true capacity during a presentation in Lahore. Sundar's support turned into the impetus that impelled Rafi from neighborhood approval to public acknowledgment. This act of pure trust denoted the beginning of an excursion that would see Rafi's name carved in the records of Bollywood's melodic history.

3. **Nearby Exhibitions and Radio stations: The Preface to Fame**

   Rafi's initial vocation was interspersed by neighborhood exhibitions and radio stations, where his voice originally grabbed the eye of music lovers. These stages gave a brief look into the crude ability that would before long catch the creative mind of the Indian entertainment world. The deep interpretations during this stage turned into an introduction to the ensemble that Rafi would coordinate on a lot more terrific scope.These neighborhood exhibitions were something beyond venturing stones; they were the pot wherein Rafi's voice was sharpened and refined. The private settings permitted him to interface with crowds, laying out the close to home reverberation that would later characterize his playback singing.

4. **Early Coordinated efforts with Less popular Arrangers**

   The mid 1940s denoted Rafi's introduction to playback singing, a period portrayed by coordinated efforts with less popular writers. While these sytheses might not have accomplished far and wide acknowledgment, they filled in as the lab where Rafi explored different avenues regarding his vocal reach and articulation. Tunes like "Tera Khilona Toota Balak" and "Yahan Badla Wafa Ka" mirrored the undeveloped phases of an ability bound to succeed sooner or later.Notwithstanding the general lack of clarity of these pieces, they exhibited Rafi's capacity to implant feeling into each note. The early hits with less popular authors established the groundwork for the particular quality that would separate Rafi in the years to come.

5. **Baiju Bawra (1952): The Naushad Cooperation**

   The true to life scene saw a seismic shift with Rafi's cooperation with the unbelievable writer Naushad. The soundtrack of "Baiju Bawra" (1952) was a melodic magnum opus that displayed the vocal ability of Rafi in the entirety of its magnificence. Tunes like "Man Tarpat Hari Darsan Ko Aaj" and "O Duniya Ke Rakhwale" became chartbusters as well as laid out Rafi as the go-to playback artist for entertainers and authors the same.The organization with Naushad was a defining moment in Rafi's vocation, denoting the solidification of his situation in the entertainment world. The progress of "Baiju Bawra" resounded a long ways past the film's story, flagging the appearance of a maestro whose voice would shape the brilliant time of Hindi film.

6. **Radiating brilliantly during the 1950s: Coordinated efforts with Eminent Arrangers**

The 1950s saw Rafi's rising to noticeable quality, with joint efforts that would characterize the soundscape of the period. His relationship with authors like S.D. Burman, Shankar-Jaikishan, and O.P. Nayyar turned into the foundation of his melodic excursion.

With S.D. Burman, Rafi made ageless tunes that caught the embodiment of the 1950s. Tunes like "Yeh Duniya Yeh Mehfil" and "Tere Simple Sapne Stomach muscle Ek Rang Hai" displayed the emotive profundity of Rafi's voice, making him the voice of an age going through huge socio-social changes.

The organization with Shankar-Jaikishan added a layer of extravagance to Rafi's collection. Perky numbers like "Yippee! Chahe Koi Mujhe Junglee Kahe" and deep interpretations like "Ehsaan Tera Hoga Mujh Standard" exhibited Rafi's adaptability, easily exploring between various states of mind and kinds.

O.P. Nayyar's pieces injected an energetic liveliness into Rafi's discography. The foot-tapping numbers from films like "Naya Daur" (1957) displayed an alternate feature of Rafi's ability, demonstrating that his voice could adjust to different melodic styles.

7. **Ghazals and Reflection Tunes: Investigating Creative Aspects**

Rafi's flexibility reached out past the domains of film music to the ghazal and reflection classes. The spirit mixing version of "Chaudhvin Ka Chand Ho" exemplified his capacity to convey profound feelings with nuance and artfulness. Ghazals permitted Rafi to investigate the subtleties of tune and verse, uncovering a milder, contemplative side of his vocal reach.

Reflection tunes turned into one more element of Rafi's creative collection. His versions in this classification, for example, "Madhuban Mein Radhika Nache Re" and "Mera Man Tera Pyasa," were not simple melodic exhibitions but rather otherworldly excursions that reverberated with the shared mindset of a profoundly strict and different country.

8. **Influence on Indian Film: Forming Social Accounts**

Rafi's initial vocation features were not restricted to the domains of music; they significantly affected the social stories of post-freedom India. The 1950s and 1960s were many years of tremendous change, and Rafi's voice turned into an impression of the country's desires, dreams, and flexibility. His tunes were something other than realistic backups; they were hymns that repeated the soul of the times. Whether it was the enthusiasm of energetic tunes like "Kar Chale Murmur Fida" or the immortal charm of heartfelt ditties like "Chaudhvin Ka Chand Ho," Rafi's voice turned into a social impetus that impacted style, language, and cultural standards.

An Introduction to Interminability

The investigation of Mohammad Rafi's initial profession features uncovers the preface to a heritage that would resound for ages. From the provincial environs of Punjab to the greatness of Mumbai's entertainment world, Rafi's process was a melodic odyssey that changed him from a neighborhood wonder into an irreplaceable asset.The coordinated efforts with unbelievable arrangers, the investigation of different classifications, and the effect on social stories denoted the early features of Rafi's profession. These years were something beyond an excursion to fame; they were a demonstration of the groundbreaking force of music and the dauntless soul of a maestro.

As the shade falls on this investigation, it abandons a melodic introduction — an orchestra that makes way for the crescendo of Rafi's celebrated lifetime. The early vocation features were not simply venturing stones; they were the structure blocks of an inheritance that would rise above time, resounding with the central cores of music lovers across the globe.

1.2 Nostalgic trip through the golden era of Hindi cinema

The brilliant period of Hindi film, spreading over generally from the last part of the 1940s to the 1960s, holds a unique spot in the hearts of cinephiles and music fans the same. It was an age described by immortal narrating, realistic craftsmanship, and, maybe most quite, the rise of tunes that have scratched themselves into the aggregate memory of a country. This nostalgic outing through the brilliant period isn't just an excursion through film history; an ensemble of tunes and recollections keep on reverberating, rising above the limits of time.

1. **The True to life Scene: A Time of Spearheading Inventiveness**

    The brilliant period saw a conjunction of true to life brightness, where movie producers, essayists, and performers teamed up to create notable works that have endured for the long haul. Visionaries like Master Dutt, Raj Kapoor, and Bimal Roy created accounts that resounded with the social texture of post-freedom India. The narrating was nuanced, digging into the complexities of human connections, cultural standards, and the aggregate goals of a recently free country.The movies of this period were not simply visual displays; they were materials on which the rich woven artwork of Indian culture unfurled. From the perfect scenes of the Himalayas to the lively roads of Mumbai, each edge was an impression of the variety and intricacy of the Indian experience. It was a time of spearheading inventiveness, where chiefs explored different avenues regarding story structures, presenting components of neo-authenticity, imagery, and social critique.

2. **The Melodic Climate: Rafi's Reverberation in Each Casing**

    Fundamental to the brilliant time's realistic sorcery was its melodic climate, and at the core of this melodic ensemble was the voice of Mohammad Rafi. Rafi's vocal imaginativeness turned into the sonic ally to the visual verse on screen. His capacity to implant each note with feeling, subtlety, and flexibility made him the quintessential playback vocalist of the time.The tunes of the brilliant period weren't simply foundation scores; they were basic to the account, each verse and song adding to the close to home scene of the film. Whether it was the heartfelt "Yeh Duniya Yeh Mehfil" from "Heer Raanjha" or the energetic "Simple Samne Wali Khidki Mein" from "Padosan," Rafi's voice became indistinguishable from the characters and stories that unfurled on screen.

3. **The Heartfelt Song: Catching the Quintessence of Affection**

   One of the characterizing highlights of the brilliant period was its capacity to catch the embodiment of sentiment such that rose above the screen. The movies of this period re-imagined the depiction of adoration, imbuing it with beautiful lyricism and immortal appeal. Rafi's voice, with its unmatched capacity to convey feelings, turned into the sonic encapsulation of affection in the entirety of its features.

   Melodies like "Chaudhvin Ka Chand Ho" from the film of a similar name and "Tere Simple Sapne Stomach muscle Ek Rang Hai" from "Guide" exemplify the heartfelt composition of the brilliant time. Rafi's interpretations conveyed the surface feelings of adoration as well as dove into the profundity of yearning, enthusiasm, and catastrophe. Every heartfelt song turned into a hymn, a melodic articulation of the fantasies and wants of an age.

4. **The Social Discourse: Melodies as Mirrors to Society**

   Past sentiment, the brilliant period's movies were vehicles for social discourse. Whether it was the investigation of cultural standards, monetary differences, or the battles of commoners, movie producers utilized their specialty to hold a mirror to society. Rafi's voice turned into the storyteller of these stories, articulating the expectations and troubles of a country experiencing significant change.Melodies like "Mera Joota Hai Japani" from "Shree 420" and "Yeh Mera Deewanapan Hai" from "Yahudi" weren't simply melodic recesses; they were hymns that resounded with the socio-political scene of the time. Rafi's capacity to pass a bunch of feelings permitted these tunes on to rise above their nearby settings, becoming immortal critiques on the human condition.

5. **The Reflection Orchestra: Reverberations of Confidence and Otherworldliness**

   The brilliant period likewise saw a rich embroidery of reflection and otherworldly melodies that additional one more layer of profundity to the realistic experience. Rafi's versions in this class, whether it was "Madhuban Mein Radhika Nache Re" from "Kohinoor" or "Mera Man Tera Pyasa" from "Speculator," became pathways to the heavenly.These reflection tunes weren't bound to strict customs; they turned into a piece of the social cognizance. Rafi's voice conveyed the enthusiasm of confidence, inspiring a feeling of otherworldliness that rose above strict limits. In a period of significant social and strict variety, these tunes turned into a bringing together power, interfacing individuals through the general language of music.

6. **The Loyalist's Song of praise: Rafi and the Country's Pride**
As India found its balance in the post-freedom years, a flood of enthusiastic enthusiasm moved throughout the country. The brilliant period saw the rise of songs of devotion that blended the enthusiastic soul, and indeed, Rafi's voice turned into the vehicle for communicating the aggregate pride and yearnings of a country.Melodies like "Kar Chale Murmur Fida" from "Haqeeqat" and "Ae Simple Watan Ke Logon" from an exceptional presentation at the Public Arena became mobilizing sobs for public pride. Rafi's capacity to imbue these tunes with feeling transformed them into more than simple pieces; they became sonic epitomes of the penances and commitment of the Indian public.

7. **Rafi's Coordinated effort with Music Maestros: An Amicable Inheritance**
The brilliant time likewise saw Rafi's coordinated efforts with incredible music authors, each adding to the orchestra of tunes that characterized the period. Whether it was the profound structures of S.D. Burman, the overflowing tunes of Shankar-Jaikishan, or the exploratory hints of R.D. Burman, Rafi flawlessly adjusted to the assorted styles of these maestros.S.D. Burman's structures like "Clamor Dhal Jaye" and "Aaj Phir Jeene Ki Tamanna Hai" exhibited the spirit blending nature of Rafi's voice. Shankar-Jaikishan's tunes, going from the lively "Hurray! Chahe Koi Mujhe Junglee Kahe" to the melancholic "Yeh Mera Prem Patra Padhkar," uncovered the profundity and adaptability of Rafi's creativity. The joint effort with R.D. Burman in the later years added a contemporary edge to Rafi's collection, delivering hits like "Mera Man Tera Pyasa" and "Chookar simple man ko."

8. **True to life Achievements: Notable Tunes and Ageless Movies**
The brilliant period gifted Hindi film with notorious melodies that are indivisible from the movies they have a place with. Rafi's voice became inseparable from these artistic achievements, and the tunes turned into a basic piece of the social inheritance. "Pyasa" (1957), "Guide" (1965), and "Mughal-e-Azam" (1960) stand as brilliant illustrations of the period's artistic splendor, with Rafi's voice adding a permanent layer of wizardry to these immortal movies."Chaudhvin Ka Chand Ho" from the film of a similar name, "Tere Simple Sapne Stomach muscle Ek Rang Hai" from "Guide," and "Ae Meri Zohra Jabeen" from "Waqt" are not tunes; they are embodiments of the true to life ethos of the brilliant time. These creations flawlessly mixed with the account, raising the profound effect of the movies and leaving a never-ending engrave on the personalities of crowds.

9. **Social Effect and Heritage: Rafi's Voice as a Period Case**

The social effect of the brilliant period stretches out past the domains of film. Rafi's voice, with its capacity to exemplify the bunch feelings of the period, turned into a period case that protected the ethos of post-freedom India. The melodies filled in as sonic markers, mirroring the developing goals, dreams, and difficulties of a country tracking down its character.Rafi's inheritance isn't bound to wistfulness; it is a living demonstration of the persevering through force of music. His tunes keep on reverberating with crowds across ages, not just as relics of the past yet as immortal articulations of the human experience. The effect of Rafi's voice goes past diversion; a social legacy enhances the embroidery of Indian legacy.

Reverberations of an Evergreen Period

The nostalgic outing through the brilliant period of Hindi film, directed by the immortal songs of Mohammad Rafi, is in excess of an excursion through a world of fond memories. A submersion into an evergreen period keeps on resounding through the passages of time. The brilliant time wasn't simply a period in film history; it was a conversion of creativity, narrating, and music that molded the social cognizance of a country.Rafi's voice, with its personal reverberation and flexibility, turned into the brilliant string winding through the complex texture of this realistic period. The heartfelt ditties, the social editorials, the reflection ensembles, and the enthusiastic songs of praise — all got comfortable with themselves in Rafi's unmatched creativity. The cooperative endeavors with music maestros and the realistic achievements made a heritage that rises above the constraints of existence.

As the shade falls on this nostalgic outing, the reverberations of Rafi's songs wait, welcoming audience members to cross the ageless scenes of a time that will always be scratched in the records of artistic and melodic history. The brilliant time stays a section in the past as well as a living demonstration of the persevering through force of workmanship to catch the human soul and mesh it into an embroidery of songs and recollections.

1.3 Significance of Rafi's collaborations with iconic composers

The meaning of Mohammad Rafi's joint efforts with famous writers in the domain of Hindi film is much the same as seeing an expert painter make a work of art on a huge material. Rafi, the maestro of playback singing, consistently explored through different melodic scenes, molding and advancing every arrangement with his unmatched vocal masterfulness. This investigation digs into the harmonious connections Rafi fashioned with incredible arrangers, disentangling the significant meaning of these joint efforts that established the groundwork for the brilliant period of Hindi film music.

1. **S.D. Burman: The Heartfelt Cooperative energy**

   The coordinated effort between Mohammad Rafi and S.D. Burman remains as a demonstration of the heartfelt cooperative energy that described the brilliant time of Hindi film. S.D. Burman, with his natural capacity to combine Indian traditional music with Western impacts, tracked down in Rafi's voice the ideal instrument to make an interpretation of his melodic vision into the real world.

Clamor Dhal Jaye and Aaj Phir Jeene Ki Tamanna Hai: Soul-blending Songs

The tune "Noise Dhal Jaye" from the film "Guide" (1965) epitomizes the enchanted that unfurled when Rafi's voice met Burman's sytheses. Rafi's interpretation, rich with profound profundity, consistently mixed with the frightful songs made by Burman. The outcome was an immortal piece that raised the true to life story as well as turned into a song of devotion of existential examination.Essentially, "Aaj Phir Jeene Ki Tamanna Hai" from the film "Guide" is one more show-stopper that features the advantageous interaction among Rafi and Burman. Rafi's spirit mixing version, implanted with a feeling of yearning and trust, reflected the hero's excursion in the film. Burman's imaginative utilization of coordination and Rafi's emotive conveyance made a melodic embroidery that resounded with crowds across ages.

Yeh Duniya Yeh Mehfil: A Song of praise of Reflection

"Yeh Duniya Yeh Mehfil" from the film "Heer Raanjha" (1970) is one more jewel that arose out of the Rafi-Burman cooperation. The tune, communicating the fleetingness of common undertakings, displayed Rafi's capacity to pass philosophical profundity on through his vocals. Burman's piece, with its strong effortlessness, supplemented Rafi's interpretation, making it a hymn of reflection and thoughtfulness.

Adaptability in Reach: Heartfelt and Lively Numbers

The Rafi-Burman organization wasn't bound to soul-blending songs alone; it traversed the whole range of human feelings. From heartfelt anthems like "Tere Simple Sapne Stomach muscle Ek Rang Hai" to lively numbers like "Chhod Do Aanchal," Rafi's adaptability tracked down its ideal match in Burman's capacity to create assorted melodic scenes.The meaning of these coordinated efforts lies in the way that every melody turned into a work of art, a demonstration of the imaginative collaboration between Rafi's vocals and Burman's sytheses. Their joint effort wasn't simply a gathering of melodic personalities; it was the formation of a heritage that keeps on charming crowds.

2. **Shankar-Jaikishan: Extravagance and Melodic Dominance**

The organization among Rafi and the melodic team Shankar-Jaikishan delivered a period of richness and melodic authority. The team's capacity to make pieces that mirrored the energy of the times tracked down an ideal divert in Rafi's dynamic vocal reach.

Yippee! Chahe Koi Mujhe Junglee Kahe: Extravagant Energy

The tune "Yippee! Chahe Koi Mujhe Junglee Kahe" from the film "Junglee" (1961) turned into a song of praise of youth and extravagance. Rafi's version caught the irresistible enthusiasm of the melody, and Shankar-Jaikishan's sythesis, with its exuberant coordination, denoted a takeoff from the regular, introducing another time of enthusiastic, foot-tapping numbers.

Ehsaan Tera Hoga Mujh Standard: Deep Sentiment

On the opposite finish of the range, the deep heartfelt anthem "Ehsaan Tera Hoga Mujh Standard" from the film "Junglee" displayed the flexibility of the Rafi-Shankar-Jaikishan coordinated effort. The delicacy in Rafi's voice, combined with the melodic wealth of Shankar-Jaikishan's organization, made an immortal piece that stays scratched in the chronicles of Hindi film music.

Mera Man Tera Pyasa: A Ghazal Moving

The ghazal "Mera Man Tera Pyasa" from the film "Speculator" (1971) is a demonstration of the trial soul of their coordinated effort. Rafi's version, injected with the heartfelt subtleties of a ghazal, exhibited his capacity to navigate different melodic kinds. Shankar-Jaikishan's exploratory way to deal with structure made this tune a special pearl in the mother lode of their coordinated efforts.

Influence on Mainstream society: Immortal Hits

The meaning of the Rafi-Shankar-Jaikishan coordinated efforts goes past individual tunes; it penetrated mainstream society. Hits like "Jeene Ke Hain Chaar Noise" from "Mujhse Shaadi Karogi" and "Aasman Se Aaya Farishta" from "A Night in Paris" became inseparable from the lively soul of the 1960s.Their coordinated efforts were not simply melodic breaks in films; they were social peculiarities that molded the soundscape of a period set apart by social unrest and social change.

3. **O.P. Nayyar: Perky Rhythms and Foot-tapping Numbers**

   The organization among Rafi and O.P. Nayyar delivered an unmistakable flavor set apart by lively rhythms and foot-tapping numbers. Nayyar's pieces, known for their novel organization and trial songs, tracked down a powerful translator in Rafi.

   Aaiye Meherbaan: Foot-tapping Rhythms

   The tune "Aaiye Meherbaan" from the film "Howrah Scaffold" (1958) is an exemplary illustration of the enchantment made when Rafi's voice met Nayyar's sytheses. The foot-tapping rhythms, combined with Rafi's dynamic version, made this melody a persevering through #1.

   Nayyar's propensity for making music that reverberated with the majority tracked down an ideal outlet in Rafi's capacity to pass richness on through his vocals.

   Yeh Desh Hai Go Jawano Ka: Enthusiastic Intensity

   One more prominent coordinated effort among Rafi and Nayyar was the enthusiastic song of devotion "Yeh Desh Hai Go Jawano Ka" from the film "Naya Daur" (1957). The tune, with its energetic organization and Rafi's intense version, turned into a mobilizing sob for public pride. The meaning of this joint effort lies in its capacity to catch the energetic enthusiasm of the times and imbue it into the melodic scene.

   Aa Jaane Jaan: A Mix of Exotic nature and Beat

"Aa Jaane Jaan" from the film "Intaquam" (1969) is a demonstration of Nayyar's trial approach and Rafi's flexibility. The tune, set apart by erotic nature and mood, displayed an alternate feature of Rafi's flexibility. Nayyar's organizations, frequently described by eccentric designs, tracked down a willing mediator in Rafi, making tunes that pushed the limits of customary film music.

Social Effect: Melodies That Characterized a Time

The meaning of the Rafi-Nayyar cooperation stretches out past the domain of individual tunes. Together, they made a melodic inheritance that characterized a time set apart by trial and error and social dynamism. Hits like "Yunhi Tum Mujhse Baat Karti Ho" from "Sachaa Jhutha" and "Zaroorat Hai Zaroorat Hai" from "Man-Mauji" became symbolic of the period's melodic outlook.

4. R.D. Burman: Contemporary Sounds and Trial and error

The cooperation among Rafi and R.D. Burman denoted a period of change in Hindi film music, described by contemporary sounds and trial and error. R.D. Burman, the melodic dissident, found in Rafi an entertainer who could adjust to the changing melodic scene of the 1970s.

Chookar Simple Man Ko: Combination of Song and Western Impacts

The tune "Chookar Simple Man Ko" from the film "Yaarana" (1981) is a great representation of the combination of song and Western impacts that characterized their coordinated effort. Rafi's emotive interpretation, combined with Burman's exploratory coordination, made a tune that reverberated with the developing preferences of the crowd. The cooperation mirrored the capacity of the two craftsmen to adjust to contemporary patterns while keeping up with the profound profundity that portrayed their previous works.

Tum Jo Mil Gaye Ho: Melancholic Sorcery

The melancholic sorcery of "Tum Jo Mil Gaye Ho" from the film "Hanste Zakhm" (1973) exhibits the profundity and development in Rafi's voice during this period of his vocation. Burman's sythesis, set apart by its spirit mixing song, gave a material to Rafi to convey a range of feelings. The meaning of this cooperation lies in its capacity to rise above the customary limits of film music and make tunes that endured over the extreme long haul.

Mehbooba: Trial and error and Development

The melody "Mehbooba" from the film "Sholay" (1975) embodies the trial and error and development that described the Rafi-R.D. Burman cooperation. The melody, with its flighty design and combination of sorts, turned into a faction exemplary. Rafi's capacity to adjust to Burman's cutting edge pieces exhibited a powerful organization that pushed the limits of customary film music.

Influence on the Business: Another Melodic Language

The Rafi-R.D. Burman coordinated effort essentially affected the music business, impacting another age of writers and audience members. Their trial and error with sounds, types, and game plans set up for a change in the melodic scene of Hindi film. Tunes like "Yeh Jo Mohabbat Hai" from "Kati Patang" and "Aaj Mausam Bada Beimaan Hai" from "Loafer" became songs of praise of an evolving time.

The Tradition of Congruity

The meaning of Mohammad Rafi's coordinated efforts with notable writers rises above the limits of film music; a tradition of concordance has made a permanent imprint on the social scene of India. Every cooperation addresses a part in the story of Hindi film, where the maestro's voice turned into the vehicle for the melodic dreams of unbelievable writers.

The Rafi-Burman organization represents the deep cooperative energy that characterized the brilliant time, with tunes that keep on summoning feelings and resound with crowds. Shankar-Jaikishan's extravagance and melodic authority tracked down articulation through Rafi's dynamic vocals, making immortal hits that characterized a time of social dynamism. O.P. Nayyar's energetic rhythms and exploratory tunes found a willing mediator in Rafi, bringing about melodies that became social peculiarities.

The cooperation with R.D. Burman denoted a period of change, where Rafi adjusted to contemporary sounds while keeping up with the profound profundity that portrayed his previous works. Together, they made a melodic language that impacted another age of performers and audience members.

The meaning of these joint efforts lies in their capacity to exemplify the ethos of their separate periods. These organizations weren't just about making hit tunes; they were tied in with winding around an embroidery of songs that turned into a basic piece of the social and social texture. Rafi's voice, with its close to home reverberation and flexibility, turned into the consistent idea interfacing assorted melodic classifications and styles.

As the reverberations of Rafi's joint efforts keep on resounding through the passages of time, they act as a wake up call of the getting through force of concordance and the extraordinary effect of music on the human experience. The tradition of Mohammad Rafi's joint efforts with notorious writers stays a demonstration of the immortal association of vocal splendor and melodic virtuoso — a heritage that proceeds to charm and rouse ages of music fans all over the planet.

Chapter 2

Versatility and Emotive Range

Adaptability and emotive reach stand as mainstays of melodic greatness, and scarcely any craftsmen epitomize these characteristics as significantly as Mohammad Rafi. In the domain of playback singing, Rafi's unmatched capacity to adjust to different types and convey a range of feelings places him without equal. This investigation digs into the multi-layered elements of Rafi's adaptability and emotive reach, disentangling the unpredictable embroidered artwork of his melodic masterfulness.

1. **The Virtuosity of Vocal Flexibility**
   Versatility Across Kinds
   Rafi's flexibility rises above the limits of kinds, enveloping traditional, society, ghazal, reflection, and famous music. His capacity to flawlessly change from a profound ghazal like "Chaudhvin Ka Chand Ho" to the musical extravagance of "Yippee! Chahe Koi Mujhe Junglee Kahe" is a demonstration of the endlessness of his vocal range. This part investigates Rafi's introductions to different melodic classifications, featuring his dominance in each.
   Traditional Ability: An Excursion through Ragas
   Rafi's traditional preparation under Ustad Bade Ghulam Ali Khan established the groundwork for his multifaceted comprehension of ragas. From the old style subtleties of "Madhuban Mein Radhika Nache Re" to the reflection profundity of "Man Tarpat Hari Darsan Ko Aaj," Rafi's versions exhibit a significant association with old style customs. This fragment dives into the old style features of Rafi's collection and their effect on his general flexibility.
   Society Articulations: Established Tunes
   The society customs of India tracked down reverberation in Rafi's voice, adding credibility to his versions. Whether it was the provincial appeal of "O Simple Sona Re" or the gritty intensity of "Jhoom Barabar Jhoom," Rafi's society articulations showed an inborn association with the social texture of the country. This

part investigates how Rafi's flexibility stretched out to catching the embodiment of society songs.

Ghazals and Commitment: Personal Articulations

Rafi's emotive reach arrived at its pinnacle in the domain of ghazals and reflection melodies. His version of ghazals like "Chaudhvin Ka Chand Ho" and reflection works of art like "Mera Man Tera Pyasa" exhibited a wonderful closeness that contacted the hearts of audience members. This section dives into Rafi's capacity to convey significant feelings in the domains of adoration and otherworldliness.

2. **Emotive Reach: A Kaleidoscope of Sentiments**

Heartfelt Reverberation: From Delicate to Energetic

Rafi's voice became inseparable from sentiment, catching the fragile subtleties of affection in its different structures. The delicacy in "Tere Simple Sapne Stomach muscle Ek Rang Hai" appears differently in relation to the enthusiastic charm of "Ae Meri Zohra Jabeen." This part investigates how Rafi's emotive reach raised heartfelt melodies to ageless articulations of affection in Hindi film.

Despairing and Yearning: Reverberations of Distress

The profundity of Rafi's emotive reach is maybe most obvious in his versions of melancholic tunes. Melodies like "Yeh Duniya Yeh Mehfil" and "Noise Dhal Jaye" reverberate with a feeling of contemplation and yearning, exhibiting Rafi's capacity to convey significant distress. This portion looks at how Rafi's voice turned into a vessel for the piercing feelings of despairing and longing.

Enthusiastic Intensity: Reverberations of Public Pride

As India explored its post-freedom character, Rafi's voice arose as an image of energetic intensity. Songs of devotion like "Kar Chale Murmur Fida" and "Ae Simple Watan Ke Logon" encapsulated penance and commitment. This segment investigates how Rafi's emotive reach stretched out to encapsulating the aggregate pride and desires of a country.

Lively Extravagance: Musical Festivals

Rafi's adaptability isn't bound to thoughtful or serious subjects; it reaches out to overflowing and energetic articulations. Tunes like "Yippee! Chahe Koi Mujhe Junglee Kahe" and "Aaiye Meherbaan" are imbued with a cadenced liveliness that features Rafi's capacity to convey satisfaction and festivity. This portion unwinds the happy features of Rafi's emotive reach.

3. **Coordinated efforts and Impact: Forming a Melodic Inheritance**

Famous Writers: An Orchestra of Virtuoso

Rafi's coordinated efforts with amazing arrangers like S.D. Burman, Shankar-Jaikishan, O.P. Nayyar, and R.D. Burman essentially added to his flexibility and emotive reach. Every coordinated effort delivered an exceptional combination of melodic virtuoso, bringing about immortal organizations. This part dives into the effect of these joint efforts on Rafi's masterfulness.

Excellent Associations: Shankar-Jaikishan and S.D. Burman

The association with Shankar-Jaikishan delivered a time of richness and melodic dominance, while the joint effort with S.D. Burman represented a deep cooperative energy. Examining explicit melodies and topical components, this portion investigates what these associations meant for Rafi's capacity to explore assorted melodic scenes.

O.P. Nayyar and R.D. Burman: Trial and error and Change

O.P. Nayyar's enthusiastic rhythms and test tunes tracked down a unique translator in Rafi, bringing about notable hits. The cooperation with R.D. Burman denoted a change into contemporary sounds and trial and error. This segment dives into how these organizations extended Rafi's flexibility and added to the advancement of his emotive reach.

Impact on Ages: An Immortal Heritage

Rafi's impact reaches out past his own period, molding the melodic scene for a long time into the future. Analyzing the effect of his adaptable voice and emotive reach on ensuing playback vocalists, this portion follows the getting through tradition of Rafi's masterfulness in the more extensive setting of Indian film music.

4. **Live Exhibitions and Inheritance: Reverberations Through Time**

Live Sorcery: Rising above Studio Limits

Rafi's live exhibitions added one more aspect to his flexibility and emotive reach. Breaking down striking live versions, this part investigates how Rafi's stage presence and suddenness displayed the quick and otherworldly characteristics of his imaginativeness.

Heritage in Contemporary Music: Reverberations in Present day Versions

The reverberations of Rafi's adaptability and emotive reach continue in contemporary music. Analyzing how current craftsmen give proper respect to Rafi's heritage, this part features the proceeded with significance of his masterfulness and the effect on the developing scene of Indian playback singing.

The Never-ending Reverberations

Mohammad Rafi's flexibility and emotive reach are not only features of his vocal ability; they address an excursion through the different scenes of human inclination. From traditional complexities to society effortlessness, from heartfelt melodies to devoted hymns, Rafi's voice crosses the whole range of human experience.

His coordinated efforts with notorious authors filled in as pots of imagination, producing immortal sytheses that keep on resounding across ages. The tradition of Rafi's imaginativeness isn't bound to the past; it lives on in the contemporary versions and the getting through influence on the melodic soul of India.

As we disentangle the layers of Rafi's flexibility and emotive reach, we experience a melodic heritage that rises above time. His voice, a melodic compass exploring the feelings of a country, makes a permanent imprint on the hearts of audience members, advising us that genuine creativity knows no limits — it reverberations through time, ever-present and never-ending.

2.1 Showcase of Rafi's versatile vocal abilities

Mohammad Rafi, the maestro of playback singing in the Indian entertainment world, remains as an exemplification of vocal flexibility. His capacity to consistently navigate different types and pass a range of feelings raised him on to the zenith of melodic creativity. This investigation digs into the multi-layered feature of Rafi's flexible vocal capacities, unwinding the enchanted that unfurled across the immense material of Hindi film music.

1. **The Old style Rhythm: Rafi's Dominance of Ragas**
   Establishment in Old style Preparing
   Rafi's excursion into the universe of music was well established in old style preparing under the tutelage of Ustad Bade Ghulam Ali Khan. This part digs into the impact of traditional music on Rafi's vocal strategies, looking at how his old style establishment turned into a foundation of his flexibility.
   Raga-based Interpretations: An Excursion Through Melodic Scales
   Rafi's control over old style ragas tracked down articulation in various creations. From the heartfelt version of "Madhuban Mein Radhika Nache Re" to the reflection enthusiasm of "Man Tarpat Hari Darsan Ko Aaj," Rafi's dominance over raga-based songs is investigated in this section, exhibiting the profundity and complexity of his traditional rhythm.

2. **Ghazals and Sufi Articulations: Rafi's Cozy Accounts**
   Ghazal as a Work of art
   The ghazal kind furnished Rafi with a stage to communicate significant feelings and multifaceted expressive stories. This segment dives into famous ghazals like "Chaudhvin Ka Chand Ho" and "Rang Aur Noor Ki Baraat," unwinding Rafi's emotive profundity in conveying the nuances of adoration, yearning, and other-worldliness.
   Sufi Dedication: Profound Reverberations
   Rafi's interpretation of Sufi creations, for example, "Mera Man Tera Pyasa" and "Na Tu Zameen Ke Liye," mirrors his capacity to inject profound enthusiasm into his vocal articulations. This section investigates how Rafi's flexible voice turned into a vessel for conveying the dedication and otherworldliness intrinsic in Sufi customs.

3. **Folkloric Artfulness: Rafi's Local Reverberation**
   Embracing Society Customs
   Rafi's adaptability stretched out to catching the quintessence of people tunes, imbuing his versions with territorial flavors. Tunes like "O Simple Sona Re" and "Jhoom Barabar Jhoom" are inspected to grandstand how Rafi easily embraced

folkloric artfulness, making a connective extension between the artistic world and various social practices.

Regional Variety: From Bhojpuri to Punjabi

Rafi's capacity to adjust his voice to various vernaculars is investigated through sytheses in local dialects. Whether singing in Bhojpuri for "Jugnu" or mixing Punjabi people components into "Luti Zindagi Aur Gham Musallat Fundamental Hoon," this fragment features Rafi's semantic adaptability.

4. **Heartfelt Dream: Rafi's Spellbinding Affection Anthems**
   Delicate Melodies: Exploring the Scene of Affection

Rafi's voice became inseparable from sentiment, and this part dives into his delicate songs that conveyed the bunch aspects of adoration. Melodies like "Tere Simple Sapne Stomach muscle Ek Rang Hai" and "Chaudhvin Ka Chand Ho" are investigated to feature Rafi's capacity to bring out heartfelt dream through his flexible vocal subtleties.

Energetic Articulations: The Profundity of Rafi's Heartfelt Collection

Moving past delicate songs, Rafi's heartfelt collection additionally enveloped energetic articulations of affection. Melodies like "Ae Meri Zohra Jabeen" and "Tum Jo Mil Gaye Ho" epitomize the profundity and power that Rafi brought to heartfelt anthems, displaying his flexibility in exploring the profound range of affection.

5. **Energetic Rhythms: Rafi's Lively Articulations**
   Perky and Lively Numbers: A Unique Exhibit

Rafi's adaptability isn't restricted to profound and scrutinizing classifications; he likewise succeeded in conveying cheery and perky numbers. Tunes like "Hurray! Chahe Koi Mujhe Junglee Kahe" and "Aaiye Mcherbaan" feature Rafi's lively articulations and his capacity to implant satisfaction and energy into his vocal exhibitions.

Celebratory Tunes: From Merriments to Move Numbers

Rafi's voice turned into a guide of festivity, with organizations that resound during celebrations and dance successions. This portion investigates how Rafi's vocal adaptability carried life to celebratory tunes, making them necessary to the glad minutes in Hindi film.

6. **Social and Enthusiastic Songs of praise: Rafi's Public Rhythm**
   Socio-political Analyses: Tunes as Mirrors to Society

Past private and heartfelt topics, Rafi's flexible voice turned into a vehicle for socio-political critiques. Melodies like "Mera Joota Hai Japani" and "Yeh Mera Deewanapan Hai" are analyzed to exhibit how Rafi's emotive reach stretched out to passing on messages about cultural standards and political scenes.

Enthusiastic Intensity: Songs of devotion of Public Pride

Rafi's commitments to enthusiastic melodies stand as a demonstration of his obligation to public pride. Famous songs of devotion like "Ae Simple Watan Ke

Logon" and "Kar Chale Murmur Fida" are investigated to feature Rafi's capacity to mix enthusiastic intensity into his vocal versions, turning into the voice of a country.

7. **Notorious Coordinated efforts: The Amicable Combination**

S.D. Burman: Deep Cooperative energy

Rafi's joint effort with S.D. Burman is analyzed in this part, featuring the profound collaboration that created immortal works of art like "Racket Dhal Jaye" and "Aaj Phir Jeene Ki Tamanna Hai." The nuanced articulations in these melodies grandstand the consistent combination of Rafi's adaptable voice with Burman's organizations.

Shankar-Jaikishan: Abundance and Melodic Authority

The extravagance and melodic dominance that obvious Rafi's coordinated effort with Shankar-Jaikishan are investigated through vivacious numbers like "Yippee! Chahe Koi Mujhe Junglee Kahe" and deep anthems like "Ehsaan Tera Hoga Mujh Standard." This segment unwinds the energetic articulations that rose up out of this powerful organization.

O.P. Nayyar and R.D. Burman: Trial and error and Advancement

Rafi's joint effort with O.P. Nayyar is analyzed with regards to foot-tapping rhythms and trial tunes, displayed in melodies like "Aaiye Meherbaan" and "Yeh Desh Hai Go Jawano Ka." The progress to contemporary sounds and trial and error with R.D. Burman is investigated through organizations like "Chookar Simple Man Ko" and "Mehbooba," representing Rafi's versatility to advancing melodic scenes.

8. **Inheritance and Impact: Reverberations Through Ages**

Persevering through Heritage: Rafi's Effect on Playback Singing

Rafi's inheritance isn't restricted to his time; it resounds through resulting ages of playback vocalists. Dissecting the impact of Rafi's adaptable vocal capacities on specialists like Sonu Nigam and Arijit Singh, this segment investigates how his creativity keeps on molding the scene of Indian playback singing.

Reverence and Recognitions: Rafi's Presence in Present day Versions

The part on present day interpretations analyzes how contemporary craftsmen give recognition to Rafi's flexible inheritance. Through instances of recognition exhibitions and covers, it becomes obvious that Rafi's impact stays a directing power for hopeful vocalists and a wellspring of motivation for reevaluations of his immortal works of art.

A Melodic Odyssey Across Sorts and Feelings

Mohammad Rafi's flexible vocal capacities comprise a hypnotizing odyssey across the tremendous range of melodic types and profound scenes. From traditional complexities to society straightforwardness, from heartfelt songs to enthusiastic hymns, Rafi's voice rises above limits, making a persevering through heritage that resounds through the ages.

His capacity to adjust to different classes, inject feelings into each note, and consistently team up with incredible writers grandstands a degree of imaginativeness that stays unmatched. Rafi's voice isn't only an assortment of notes and verses; an immortal story catches the pith of the human involvement with all its wealth and intricacy.

As we return to the feature of Rafi's flexible vocal capacities, we end up drenched in an ensemble that goes past the bounds of reality — an orchestra that keeps on reverberating, motivate, and charm audience members across ages. The enchantment of Rafi's voice lives on, propagating the tradition of a genuine melodic maestro who everlastingly stays in the hearts of music fans around the world.

2.2 Analysis of his emotive range in various genres

Mohammad Rafi's name is inseparable from profound profundity and adaptability in the domain of Indian playback singing. His capacity to convey a large number of feelings, from the delicate subtleties of adoration to the piercing profundities of distress, has made a permanent imprint on the chronicles of Hindi film music. This investigation dives into the emotive scope of Rafi's voice, taking apart its subtleties and effect across different types, and unwinding the profound embroidered artwork that he wove through his renowned lifetime.

1. **Heartfelt Dream: Delicate Murmurs and Energetic Rhythms**
   Delicate Songs: Catching the Substance of Affection
   Rafi's emotive reach in heartfelt ditties is unrivaled. Whether it's the fantastic "Tere Simple Sapne Stomach muscle Ek Rang Hai" or the spirit blending "Chaudhvin Ka Chand Ho," Rafi can imbue delicacy into his voice, making a close association with the audience. This segment investigates how Rafi's emotive reach in heartfelt tunes lifts the pith of adoration to heavenly levels.
   Enthusiastic Articulations: The Force of Rafi's Heartfelt Collection
   Moving past delicate melodies, Rafi's voice digs into the domains of extraordinary enthusiasm. Tunes like "Ae Meri Zohra Jabeen" and "Tum Jo Mil Gaye Ho" grandstand an alternate feature of his emotive reach, where he conveys significant feelings with an enrapturing power. This portion analyzes the subtleties of Rafi's conveyance in these enthusiastic articulations of affection.

2. **Melancholic Songs: Reverberations of Distress and Yearning**
   Profundity of Distress: Rafi's Strong Versions
   Rafi's emotive reach stretches out to the domain of despairing, where he turns into the voice of distress and longing. Tunes like "Yeh Duniya Yeh Mehfil" and "Clamor Dhal Jaye" are impactful instances of how Rafi implants his voice with a profundity of feeling that resounds with audience members on a significant level. This segment dissects the profound subtleties in Rafi's versions of melancholic songs.
   Yearning and Reflection: Rafi's Thoughtful Accounts
   Yearning and thoughtfulness track down a powerful articulation in Rafi's

emotive reach. The intelligent nature of his voice in melodies like "Tere Bina Zindagi Se" and "Maine Pucha Chand Se" conveys a feeling of longing and thought. This portion analyzes how Rafi's voice turns into a vessel for reflective stories, adding layers of feeling to the expressive organizations.

3. **Cheerful Rhythm: Celebratory Articulations and Perky Rhythms**
Celebratory Tunes: Rafi's Voice in Merriments

Rafi's emotive reach isn't bound to thoughtful or sad subjects; it stretches out to upbeat festivals. Tunes like "Hurray! Chahe Koi Mujhe Junglee Kahe" and "Aaiye Meherbaan" grandstand the richness and energetic side of Rafi's voice. This part investigates how he implants bliss and energy into his vocal exhibitions during celebratory tunes.

Lively Rhythms: Elements in Rafi's Playful Numbers

The lively and dynamic characteristics in Rafi's voice sparkle in perky and cadenced structures. From foot-tapping numbers like "Aaj Mausam Bada Beimaan Hai" to the exuberant "Yunhi Tum Mujhse Baat Karti Ho," Rafi's emotive reach stretches out to the dynamic and vivacious rhythms of energetic rhythms. This section dissects how Rafi's voice turns into a wellspring of irresistible enthusiasm in peppy creations.

4. **Reflection Dedication: Profound Respect and Sufi Reverberations**
Otherworldly Veneration: Rafi's Voice in Reflection Accounts

Rafi's emotive reach tracks down reverberation in reflection tunes, where he turns into the vehicle for profound stories. Tunes like "Man Tarpat Hari Darsan Ko Aaj" and "Sukh Ke Sab Saathi Dukh Mein Na Koi" feature the profound otherworldly association in Rafi's voice. This part takes apart the emotive subtleties that make Rafi's versions in reflection types significantly moving.

Sufi Reverberations: Mysterious Aspects in Rafi's Voice

The Sufi custom tracks down articulation in Rafi's emotive reach, where he mixes his voice with otherworldliness and dedication. Melodies like "Na Tu Zameen Ke Liye" and "Mera Man Tera Pyasa" become channels for the magical components of Sufi verse. This fragment dissects how Rafi catches the profound embodiment of Sufi creations with his emotive vocals.

5. **Social Editorial: Rafi's Voice as a Mirror to Society**
Socio-political Stories: Rafi as a Voice of Discourse

Rafi's emotive reach stretches out past private and heartfelt subjects to include socio-political discourses. Tunes like "Mera Joota Hai Japani" and "Yeh Mera Deewanapan Hai" become mirrors to society, where Rafi turns into a voice of discourse and reflection. This part takes apart the way that Rafi passes cultural messages on through his emotive vocal conveyances.

Enthusiastic Enthusiasm: Songs of devotion of Public Pride

Rafi's emotive reach arrives at its peak in enthusiastic melodies, where he turns into the voice of a country. Famous songs of praise like "Ae Simple Watan Ke

Logon" and "Kar Chale Murmur Fida" are broke down to feature how Rafi's voice turns into an image of enthusiastic enthusiasm, summoning pride and devotion. This fragment analyzes the emotive subtleties that make Rafi's versions in enthusiastic classifications significantly effective.

6. Cooperative Ensemble: The Effect of Unbelievable Arrangers

S.D. Burman: Heartfelt Collaboration in Close to home Articulations

The coordinated effort among Rafi and S.D. Burman is investigated with regards to profound articulations. Heartfelt versions like "Commotion Dhal Jaye" and "Aaj Phir Jeene Ki Tamanna Hai" grandstand the consistent combination of Rafi's emotive reach with Burman's structures. This part dissects how close to home subtleties are elevated through the amicable cooperative energy of this joint effort.

Shankar-Jaikishan: Close to home Abundance and Melodic Authority

Close to home abundance and melodic dominance portray Rafi's joint effort with Shankar-Jaikishan. Enthusiastic numbers like "Yippee! Chahe Koi Mujhe Junglee Kahe" and deep songs like "Ehsaan Tera Hoga Mujh Standard" are taken apart to feature the close to home profundity delivered through this organization. This portion disentangles the close to home articulations in Rafi's voice under the melodic direction of Shankar-Jaikishan.

O.P. Nayyar and R.D. Burman: Trial and error and Profound Development

The emotive scope of Rafi's voice takes on exploratory aspects in a joint effort with O.P. Nayyar and R.D. Burman. Enthusiastic rhythms and exploratory tunes in melodies like "Aaiye Meherbaan" and "Mehbooba" exhibit Rafi's flexibility to advancing melodic scenes. This segment dissects the close to home advancement delivered by Rafi as a team with these famous writers.

The Getting through Reverberations of Rafi's Emotive Reach

Mohammad Rafi's emotive reach is a kaleidoscope of feelings that rises above the limits of sorts. His voice is a material that paints the whole range of human sentiments — from the fragile strokes of adoration to the striking strokes of enthusiasm. Through the investigation of Rafi's emotive reach across different kinds, it becomes clear that his voice is an immortal vessel that keeps on bringing out feelings, reverberate with audience members, and leave a persevering through influence on the melodic scene.

Rafi's capacity to flawlessly adjust to various profound scenes and team up with unbelievable writers grandstands a degree of creativity that stays unmatched. His voice turns into a conductor for the statement of widespread feelings, making him a playback vocalist as a the perplexing well as a narrator stories of human encounters.

As we disentangle the profound embroidery woven by Rafi's voice, we wind up drenched in an orchestra of sentiments that goes past the limits of reality — an ensemble that keeps on reverberating, rouse, and charm audience members across ages. The getting through reverberations of Rafi's emotive reach act as a demonstration of the everlasting tradition of a melodic maestro whose voice rises above simple tunes and turns into a timeless wellspring of close to home association for music fans around the world.

2.3 Impact of Rafi's voice in conveying diverse emotions

Mohammad Rafi's voice isn't only a hear-able encounter; a close to home odyssey rises above time and resounds with the most profound openings of the human spirit. Across a vocation that spread over many years, Rafi arose as a playback vocalist as well as a maestro fit for articulating a bunch of feelings with unmatched artfulness. This investigation digs into the significant effect of Rafi's voice, taking apart its capacity to convey different feelings and unwinding the diverse layers that characterize his getting through heritage.

1. **The Delicate Stroke of Adoration: Rafi's Heartfelt Reverberation**
   Murmurs of Delicacy: Personal Articulations in Heartfelt Numbers
   Rafi's effect in conveying the subtleties of affection is exemplified by the delicacy he imbues into heartfelt anthems. Tunes like "Tere Simple Sapne Stomach muscle Ek Rang Hai" and "Chaudhvin Ka Chand Ho" feature Rafi's capacity to stroke the audience's heart with delicate murmurs of adoration. This part dissects the profound effect of Rafi's voice in making a close association through heartfelt tunes.

   Enthusiastic Rhythms: The Force of Rafi's Heartfelt Collection
   Moving past delicate melodies, Rafi's voice digs into the domains of extreme enthusiasm. Melodies like "Ae Meri Zohra Jabeen" and "Tum Jo Mil Gaye Ho" grandstand an alternate feature of his emotive reach, where he conveys significant feelings with an enamoring force. This section analyzes the close to home subtleties in Rafi's conveyance in these energetic articulations of adoration.

2. **The Strong Profundities of Distress: Rafi's Authority in Despairing**
   Articulations of Distress: Significant Feeling in Melancholic Songs
   Rafi's voice turns into a vessel for the profundities of distress and longing in melancholic songs. Tunes like "Yeh Duniya Yeh Mehfil" and "Clamor Dhal Jaye" reverberate with a significant feeling of thoughtfulness. This segment breaks down the profound effect of Rafi's voice in conveying the strong profundities of distress and the contemplative accounts that characterize these creations.

   Yearning and Reflection: Rafi's Voice as a Guide of Contemplation
   Yearning and contemplation track down an impactful articulation in Rafi's emotive reach. The intelligent nature of his voice in tunes like "Tere Bina Zindagi Se" and "Maine Pucha Chand Se" conveys a feeling of longing and consideration. This portion analyzes how Rafi's voice turns into a reference point for thoughtful stories, adding layers of feeling to the expressive creations.

3. **Blissful Rhythm: Celebratory Articulations and Perky Rhythms**
   Rhythms of Delight: Imbuing Festivities with Rafi's Voice
   Rafi's voice isn't restricted to reflective or troubled subjects; it stretches out

to upbeat festivals. Tunes like "Hurray! Chahe Koi Mujhe Junglee Kahe" and "Aaiye Meherbaan" grandstand the abundance and fun loving side of Rafi's voice. This part investigates how he mixes delight and energy into his vocal exhibitions during celebratory tunes.

Lively Rhythms: Elements in Rafi's Peppy Numbers

The lively and dynamic characteristics in Rafi's voice sparkle in energetic and musical pieces. From foot-tapping numbers like "Aaj Mausam Bada Beimaan Hai" to the vivacious "Yunhi Tum Mujhse Baat Karti Ho," Rafi's emotive reach stretches out to the energetic and enthusiastic rhythms of fun loving rhythms. This section breaks down how Rafi's voice turns into a wellspring of irresistible enthusiasm in cheery sytheses.

4. **Otherworldly Respect and Enchanted Reverberations: Rafi's Reflection Aspects**

Heartfelt Stories: Rafi's Voice in Reflection Structures

Rafi's emotive reach tracks down reverberation in reflection melodies, where he turns into the mode for profound accounts. Melodies like "Man Tarpat Hari Darsan Ko Aaj" and "Sukh Ke Sab Saathi Dukh Mein Na Koi" grandstand the profound otherworldly association in Rafi's voice. This segment analyzes the emotive subtleties that make Rafi's versions in reflection classes significantly moving.

Mysterious Reverberations: Sufi Aspects in Rafi's Voice

The Sufi custom tracks down articulation in Rafi's emotive reach, where he mixes his voice with mystery and commitment. Melodies like "Na Tu Zameen Ke Liye" and "Mera Man Tera Pyasa" become courses for the enchanted components of Sufi verse. This fragment breaks down how Rafi catches the otherworldly embodiment of Sufi creations with his emotive vocals.

5. **Social Discourse: Rafi's Voice as a Mirror to Society**

Socio-political Reflections: Melodies as Mirrors to Society

Rafi's emotive reach stretches out past private and heartfelt subjects to include socio-political discourses. Melodies like "Mera Joota Hai Japani" and "Yeh Mera Deewanapan Hai" become mirrors to society, where Rafi turns into a voice of editorial and reflection. This segment analyzes how Rafi passes cultural messages on through his emotive vocal conveyances.

Enthusiastic Intensity: Songs of praise of Public Pride

Rafi's emotive reach arrives at its pinnacle in energetic tunes, where he turns into the voice of a country. Famous songs of praise like "Ae Simple Watan Ke Logon" and "Kar Chale Murmur Fida" are examined to grandstand how Rafi's voice turns into an image of devoted enthusiasm, summoning pride and commitment. This section takes apart the emotive subtleties that make Rafi's versions in energetic types significantly effective.

6. Cooperative Orchestra: Close to home Effect in Amazing Coordinated efforts

S.D. Burman: Close to home Cooperative energy in Melodic Articulations

The joint effort among Rafi and S.D. Burman is investigated with regards to profound articulations. Profound interpretations like "Commotion Dhal Jaye" and "Aaj Phir Jeene Ki Tamanna Hai" feature the consistent combination of Rafi's emotive reach with Burman's arrangements. This segment dissects how profound subtleties are increased through the agreeable cooperative energy of this coordinated effort.

Shankar-Jaikishan: Close to home Abundance and Melodic Authority

Close to home abundance and melodic authority portray Rafi's coordinated effort with Shankar-Jaikishan. Vivacious numbers like "Yippee! Chahe Koi Mujhe Junglee Kahe" and deep numbers like "Ehsaan Tera Hoga Mujh Standard" are analyzed to grandstand the close to home profundity delivered through this association. This section unwinds the close to home articulations in Rafi's voice under the melodic direction of Shankar-Jaikishan.

O.P. Nayyar and R.D. Burman: Trial and error and Profound Development

The emotive scope of Rafi's voice takes on trial aspects as a team with O.P. Nayyar and R.D. Burman. Enthusiastic rhythms and trial tunes in melodies like "Aaiye Meherbaan" and "Mehbooba" grandstand Rafi's flexibility to developing melodic scenes. This segment breaks down the close to home development delivered by Rafi as a team with these notable writers.

Reverberations of Feeling that Rise above Time

The effect of Mohammad Rafi's voice in passing different feelings is a confirmation on to the significant imaginativeness implanted in each note he sang. His voice isn't just a vehicle for songs; it's a conductor for the whole range of human feelings. From the delicate stroke of affection to the strong profundities of distress, from blissful festivals to profound reflections, Rafi's voice reverberates with a general quality that rises above social and fleeting limits.

The profound effect of Rafi's voice lies in capacity to bring out sentiments are both individual and group. Every interpretation turns into a common encounter, a second when audience members interface with the crude, unfiltered articulations of the human heart. His coordinated efforts with unbelievable writers further advanced the profound woven artwork, making immortal works of art that keep on mixing the profundities of the spirit.

As we consider the effect of Rafi's voice, we wind up submerged in a sonic excursion that crosses the scenes of the human experience. His voice stays a timeless reverberation, a demonstration of the persevering through force of music to express the indescribable and to resound with the actual quintessence of being human. Rafi's effect isn't restricted to a period; it resonates through the halls of time, making a permanent imprint on the hearts of audience members and guaranteeing that his voice remains forever implanted in the shared awareness of music sweethearts around the world.

Chapter 3

Musical Synergy with Legendary Composers

The craft of playback singing in the Indian entertainment world isn't just about the vocalist's voice; it's a cooperative dance between the artist and the writer. Mohammad Rafi, a symbol in the domain of playback singing, produced unmatched melodic collaborations with unbelievable authors, making ageless magnum opuses that keep on reverberating through the passages of time. This investigation dives into the significant coordinated efforts that characterized Rafi's imaginative excursion, disentangling the consonant embroidery woven with authors like S.D. Burman, Shankar-Jaikishan, O.P. Nayyar, and R.D. Burman.

1. **S.D. Burman: Heartfelt Collaboration and Ageless Works of art**
   Initiation of a Cooperation: Supporting a Melodic Bond
   Rafi's coordinated effort with the maestro S.D. Burman denoted the initiation of a melodic excursion that would resound through ages. The underlying years saw the making of profound versions like "Yeh Jo Mohabbat Hai" and "Noise Dhal Jaye," establishing the groundwork for an organization that would yield immortal works of art. This segment investigates the beginning of their coordinated effort, dissecting the melodic elements that characterized the profound collaboration among Rafi and S.D. Burman.
   Famous Tunes and Topical Investigations: An Inventive Odyssey
   The inventive odyssey of Rafi and S.D. Burman dives into explicit tunes and topical components that described their joint effort. Melodies like "Aaj Phir Jeene Ki Tamanna Hai" and "Chhodo Kal Ki Baatein" grandstand the adaptability and profound profundity they brought to their pieces. This portion investigates how Rafi's voice turned into the vessel for S.D. Burman's songs, making notable pieces that turned into the soundtrack of a period.
   Development of Style and Sound: A Melodic Kaleidoscope
   As their cooperation developed, Rafi and S.D. Burman wandered into new

regions of melodic style and sound. From the enthusiastic rhythms of "O Simple Sona Re" to the spirit mixing "Zindagi Ke Safar Mein," this part dissects the development of their cooperative style. It dives into how Rafi's versatility and S.D. Burman's inventive structures made a melodic kaleidoscope that charmed crowds.

Tradition of the Rafi-S.D. Burman Joint effort: Ageless Effect

The effect of Rafi's cooperation with S.D. Burman reaches out a long ways past their dynamic years. Examining the getting through tradition of their work, this section investigates how their arrangements keep on resounding with audience members and impact resulting ages of artists. From heartfelt melodies to deep anthems, the Rafi-S.D. Burman coordinated effort remains as a demonstration of the immortal idea of their imaginative commitments.

2. **Shankar-Jaikishan: Abundance and Melodic Authority**

Time of Extravagance: A Unique Organization Uncovered

Rafi's coordinated effort with the powerful couple Shankar-Jaikishan denoted a time of richness and melodic authority. Fiery numbers like "Yippee! Chahe Koi Mujhe Junglee Kahe" and profound melodies like "Ehsaan Tera Hoga Mujh Standard" exhibited the flexibility of Rafi's voice under the melodic direction of Shankar-Jaikishan. This segment investigates the elements of their cooperation, featuring the extravagance that characterized their melodic association.

Famous Tunes and Energetic Articulations: The Shankar-Jaikishan Sorcery

The sorcery of Shankar-Jaikishan's pieces tracked down an energetic articulation through Rafi's voice. Explicit tunes like "Jeene Ke Hain Chaar Clamor" and "Ae Phoolon Ki Rani" embody the reach and liveliness they brought to Hindi film music. This section dives into the notable tunes that rose up out of their cooperation, disentangling the subtleties that made every piece a magnum opus.

Investigation of Styles: From Sentiment to Festivity

Rafi's joint effort with Shankar-Jaikishan included a wide range of melodic styles, from heartfelt songs to celebratory tunes. Breaking down the variety in their collection, this part investigates how Rafi consistently explored through various styles, turning into the voice that could convey both delicate feelings and glad festivals. The elaborate investigation inside their joint effort turns into a point of convergence of conversation.

Heritage and Proceeded with Impact: The Reverberation of Ageless Hits

The tradition of Rafi's cooperation with Shankar-Jaikishan keeps on resonating in the melodic scene. Inspecting the proceeded with impact of their ageless hits, this section dives into how contemporary specialists give proper respect to the Rafi-Shankar-Jaikishan wizardry. The persevering through effect of their joint effort becomes obvious as their organizations are returned to and reworked in present day times.

3. **O.P. Nayyar and R.D. Burman: Trial and error and Progress**
O.P. Nayyar: Lively Rhythms and Test Songs
The cooperation among Rafi and O.P. Nayyar delivered an unmistakable sound described by enthusiastic rhythms and test songs. Tunes like "Aaiye Meherbaan" and "Yeh Desh Hai Go Jawano Ka" feature the foot-tapping numbers that rose up out of this joint effort. This segment investigates how Rafi's voice turned into the unique translator of Nayyar's exploratory and musical arrangements.

R.D. Burman: Change into Contemporary Sounds
The change into contemporary sounds denoted Rafi's coordinated effort with R.D. Burman. Tunes like "Chookar Simple Man Ko" and "Mehbooba" embody the trial and error and advancement that characterized this period of their joint effort. This fragment breaks down how Rafi adjusted to the developing melodic scenes under the direction of R.D. Burman, exhibiting his adaptability in exploring the change.

Investigation of Classifications and Topics: The Variety in Articulation
The coordinated effort with O.P. Nayyar and R.D. Burman permitted Rafi to investigate assorted types and topical components. From the energetic "Yunhi Tum Mujhse Baat Karti Ho" to the thoughtful "Tum Jo Mil Gaye Ho," this part analyzes the broadness of their cooperative articulation. It investigates how Rafi's voice turned into the material for a horde of feelings and kinds, displaying his capacity to adjust to the consistently changing scene of Hindi film music.

Heritage and Impact: Adjusting to Changing Tides
The tradition of Rafi's cooperation with O.P. Nayyar and R.D. Burman lies in the hits they made as well as in the impact it applied on resulting melodic patterns. Investigating the proceeded with reverberation of their pieces, this fragment investigates how Rafi's voice adjusted to the changing tides of the music business and made a permanent imprint on the developing soundscape.

4. **Reverence and Recognitions: Rafi's Presence in Present day Versions**

Getting through Heritage: Rafi's Effect on Playback Singing
Rafi's heritage rises above his dynamic years, impacting ensuing ages of playback artists. This part dissects the effect of Rafi's vocal ability on craftsmen like Sonu Nigam and Arijit Singh, investigating how his style and emotive reach keep on forming the scene of Indian playback singing. The persevering through tradition of Rafi's creativity turns into a focal point through which we inspect the developing idea of the playback singing practice.

Reverence and Recognitions: Rafi's Presence in Present day Versions
Contemporary specialists give recognition to Rafi through ardent accolades and reevaluations of his immortal works of art. Looking at explicit occurrences of present day versions, this part exhibits how Rafi's impact stays a directing power for hopeful vocalists and a wellspring of motivation for reconsidering his notable melodies. The

persevering through presence of Rafi's voice in present day versions turns into a demonstration of the immortal nature of his imaginativeness.

A Heritage Carved as one

Mohammad Rafi's imaginative excursion through joint efforts with unbelievable writers remains as a demonstration of the force of melodic collaboration. The harmonies made between Rafi's voice and the creations of S.D. Burman, Shankar-Jaikishan, O.P. Nayyar, and R.D. Burman rose above the limits of time, making an inheritance that keeps on reverberating with crowds around the world.

Rafi's capacity to flawlessly adjust to various melodic styles and explore through different topical components exhibited a degree of masterfulness that stays unrivaled. His joint efforts were not only organizations between a vocalist and writers; they were discussions between heartfelt voices and creative personalities, bringing about an ensemble that rose above the restrictions of individual imaginativeness.

As we return to the symphonious embroidery woven by Rafi and unbelievable writers, we end up drenched in a melodic odyssey that traverses many years. The persevering through effect of these joint efforts lies in the hits they delivered as well as in the close to home reverberation they made. Rafi's voice, similar to an immortal instrument, turned into the vehicle through which the virtuoso of these writers found articulation, abandoning a heritage carved in the harmonies of melodic history.

3.1 Highlighting collaborations with S.D. Burman, Shankar-Jaikishan, and R.D. Burman

The historical backdrop of Indian playback singing is embellished with lights, and among them, Mohammad Rafi remains as an encapsulation of melodic brightness. Fundamental to Rafi's getting through inheritance are his coordinated efforts with amazing authors who molded the scene of Hindi film music. S.D. Burman, Shankar-Jaikishan, and R.D. Burman — each a maestro by their own doing — wove a melodic embroidery with Rafi that keeps on resounding across ages. This investigation digs into the consonant splendor of Rafi's coordinated efforts with these notorious authors, revealing insight into the one of a kind elements that birthed immortal works of art.

1. **S.D. Burman: Deep Cooperative energy and the Beginning of a Heritage**
   Origin of the Coordinated effort: An Intersection of Melodic Spirits
   The excursion of Rafi's joint effort with S.D. Burman started in a period that established the groundwork for the brilliant time of Hindi film music. The underlying years saw the rise of heartfelt interpretations like "Yeh Jo Mohabbat Hai" and "Commotion Dhal Jaye," making way for a cooperation that would characterize a period. This segment investigates the beginning of their melodic organization, accentuating the conjunction of two melodic spirits.
   Famous Tunes and Topical Investigations: Exploring Profound Scenes
   The Rafi-S.D. Burman cooperation unfurled like a melodic adventure, with every sythesis portraying an exceptional story. Tunes like "Aaj Phir Jeene Ki

Tamanna Hai" and "Chhodo Kal Ki Baatein" exhibited the adaptability and close to home profundity they brought to their arrangements. This portion dives into the topical investigations that characterized their cooperation, exhibiting how Rafi's voice turned into the vehicle for Burman's melodic articulations.

Development of Style and Sound: An Amicable Development

As their organization developed, Rafi and S.D. Burman wandered into new domains of melodic style and sound. From the enthusiastic rhythms of "O Simple Sona Re" to the spirit mixing "Zindagi Ke Safar Mein," this part dissects the development of their cooperative style. It dives into how Rafi's versatility and S.D. Burman's creative sytheses made an amicable development that charmed crowds.

Tradition of the Rafi-S.D. Burman Cooperation: Reverberations of Immortality

The effect of Rafi's cooperation with S.D. Burman reaches out a long ways past their dynamic years. Examining the persevering through tradition of their work, this section investigates how their organizations keep on resounding with audience members and impact resulting ages of performers. The Rafi-S.D. Burman joint effort remains as an immortal demonstration of the creative commitments that formed the brilliant time of Hindi film music.

2. **Shankar-Jaikishan: Musical Wonders and the Dance of Songs**

Time of Richness: A Powerful Organization Disclosed

The melodic scene of the 1950s and 1960s saw the rise of the unique couple, Shankar-Jaikishan, who teamed up with Rafi to make an ensemble of richness and melodic dominance. Lively numbers like "Hurray! Chahe Koi Mujhe Junglee Kahe" and deep ditties like "Ehsaan Tera Hoga Mujh Standard" displayed the flexibility of Rafi's voice under the melodic direction of Shankar-Jaikishan. This segment investigates the elements of their joint effort, featuring the abundance that characterized their melodic organization.

Notorious Melodies and Lively Articulations: The Shankar-Jaikishan Enchantment

The sorcery of Shankar-Jaikishan's pieces tracked down dynamic articulation through Rafi's voice. Explicit tunes like "Jeene Ke Hain Chaar Noise" and "Ae Phoolon Ki Rani" represent the reach and energy they brought to Hindi film music. This portion digs into the famous melodies that rose up out of their coordinated effort, unwinding the subtleties that made every creation a magnum opus.

Investigation of Styles: From Sentiment to Festivity

Rafi's joint effort with Shankar-Jaikishan incorporated a wide range of melodic styles, from heartfelt songs to celebratory tunes. Examining the variety in their collection, this part investigates how Rafi consistently explored through various styles, turning into the voice that could convey both delicate feelings and euphoric festivals. The elaborate investigation inside their cooperation turns into a point of convergence of conversation.

Inheritance and Proceeded with Impact: The Reverberation of Immortal Hits

The tradition of Rafi's joint effort with Shankar-Jaikishan keeps on resonating in the melodic scene. Analyzing the proceeded with impact of their ageless hits, this section dives into how contemporary specialists give proper respect to the Rafi-Shankar-Jaikishan enchantment. The persevering through effect of their joint effort becomes obvious as their creations are returned to and reconsidered in current times.

3. R.D. Burman: Development, Progress, and Contemporary Sounds

Change into Contemporary Sounds: R.D. Burman's Sonic Transformation

The melodic scene went through a seismic change during the 1970s, and Rafi's co-operation with R.D. Burman denoted a change into contemporary sounds. Melodies like "Chookar Simple Man Ko" and "Mehbooba" represent the trial and error and development that characterized this period of their coordinated effort. This segment dissects how Rafi adjusted to the developing melodic scenes under the direction of R.D. Burman, displaying his flexibility in exploring the change.

Investigation of Types and Subjects: The Variety in Articulation

The cooperation with R.D. Burman permitted Rafi to investigate different classifications and topical components. From the lively "Yunhi Tum Mujhse Baat Karti Ho" to the contemplative "Tum Jo Mil Gaye Ho," this part takes apart the expansiveness of their cooperative articulation. It investigates how Rafi's voice turned into the material for a heap of feelings and classifications, displaying his capacity to adjust to the consistently changing scene of Hindi film music.

Heritage and Impact: Adjusting to Changing Tides

The tradition of Rafi's joint effort with R.D. Burman lies in the hits they made as well as in the impact it applied on resulting melodic patterns. Breaking down the proceeded with reverberation of their pieces, this section investigates how Rafi's voice adjusted to the changing tides of the music business and made a permanent imprint on the advancing soundscape.

A Victorious Crescendo in Melodic History

Taking everything into account, Mohammad Rafi's coordinated efforts with S.D. Burman, Shankar-Jaikishan, and R.D. Burman address a victorious crescendo throughout the entire existence of Hindi film music. The consonant brightness that rose up out of these associations changed the true to life scene, making a permanent imprint on the hearts of millions of audience members.

The cooperation with S.D. Burman, portrayed by profound cooperative energy and topical investigations, characterized the brilliant time of Hindi film music. Shankar-Jaikishan implanted richness and dynamic quality into Rafi's collection, making immortal works of art that keep on being praised. The change into contemporary sounds with R.D. Burman denoted a sonic insurgency, displaying Rafi's flexibility and the couple's capacity to shape melodic patterns.

The tradition of these coordinated efforts isn't bound to sentimentality; it lives on in the proceeded with effect on contemporary music. The getting through reverberation of Rafi's voice, combined with the ageless creations of these maestros, guarantees that their aggregate effect rises above ages. As we ponder the consonant brightness of Rafi's joint efforts, we end up submerged in an ensemble that reverberations through time — a demonstration of the getting through force of music to shape feelings and interface individuals across periods.

3.2 Examination of the magical synergy between Rafi's voice and timeless compositions

In the records of Indian playback singing, not many names reverberate with a similar immortal reverberation as Mohammad Rafi. A maestro whose vocal ability rose above simple song, Rafi's voice tracked down its most genuine articulation in the enchanted collaboration with immortal sytheses. This investigation dives into the speculative chemistry that unfurled when Rafi's spirit blending voice met songs that endured for an extremely long period, disentangling the layers of close to home profundity and imaginative splendor implanted in these coordinated efforts.

1. **Revealing the Melodic Material: Rafi's Voice as an Instrument of Feeling**
   Rafi's Flexibility: A Chameleon in Melodic Scenes
   Rafi's voice, frequently portrayed as a chameleon in melodic scenes, had an uncommon flexibility that permitted him to cross the whole range of human feelings. From the delicate subtleties of affection to the significant profundities of distress, Rafi's voice turned into an instrument fit for conveying the most perplexing shades of feeling. This segment investigates the multi-layered nature of Rafi's vocal capacities, making way for the assessment of his supernatural cooperative energy with ageless structures.
   The Instrument of Articulation: Rafi as a Channel of Feeling
   Past the specialized brightness of his voice, Rafi arose as a conductor of feeling. His capacity to mix each note with veritable inclination raised his versions past simple melodic exhibitions. This portion dives into how Rafi's voice turned into an instrument of articulation, catching the actual quintessence of the feelings implanted in the creations he deciphered.

2. **Immortal Organizations: The Heartbeat of a Time**
   The Pith of Agelessness: Melodic Arrangements That Rise above Periods
   Immortal organizations are something other than tunes; they are social relics that catch the ethos of a time. The cooperation among Rafi and incredible writers created a gold mine of such sytheses that keep on reverberating across ages.
   This part presents the pith of immortality and the job these pieces play in

forming the melodic story of Hindi film.

Notable Arrangers: Modelers of Melodic Splendor

Behind each immortal arrangement lies the virtuoso of notable writers who molded the predetermination of Hindi film music. Any semblance of S.D. Burman, Shankar-Jaikishan, and R.D. Burman delivered tunes as well as whole melodic scenes that turned into the background of a period. This section gives an outline of these amazing writers and their commitments to the melodic heritage imparted to Rafi.

3. **S.D. Burman's Heartfelt Songs: The Beautiful Marriage of Voice and Tune Initiation of a Melodic Adventure: Rafi and S.D. Burman's Spearheading Association**

The coordinated effort among Rafi and S.D. Burman denoted the initiation of a melodic adventure that would characterize the brilliant time of Hindi film music. Melodies like "Yeh Jo Mohabbat Hai" and "Noise Dhal Jaye" exemplified the lovely marriage of Rafi's voice with S.D. Burman's profound tunes. This segment unwinds the subtleties of their spearheading organization, investigating how every version turned into an immortal show-stopper.

Soul-Mixing Songs: Rafi and S.D. Burman's Investigation of Affection and Yearning

The wizardry among Rafi and S.D. Burman tracked down pinnacle in soul-blending anthems investigated the intricacies of adoration and yearning. Melodies like "Aaj Phir Jeene Ki Tamanna Hai" and "Chhodo Kal Ki Baatein" exhibited an ideal mixture of Rafi's emotive conveyance and S.D. Burman's suggestive structures. This fragment takes apart the close to home reverberation implanted in these ageless melodies.

Development of Style: Rafi's Versatile Virtuoso and S.D. Burman's Melodic Advancement

The advancement of Rafi and S.D. Burman's cooperation reflected the changing tides of melodic style. From the traditional appeal of "O Simple Sona Re" to the thoughtful "Zindagi Ke Safar Mein," this segment examines how Rafi's versatile virtuoso mixed flawlessly with S.D. Burman's melodic development, bringing about a different and captivating collection.

4. **Shankar-Jaikishan's Musical Splendor: Vigorous Rhythms and Melodic Sorcery**

Dynamic Couple: Rafi and Shankar-Jaikishan's Melodic Odyssey

The time of abundance unfolded with the coordinated effort of Rafi and the unique couple, Shankar-Jaikishan. Their melodic odyssey created fiery rhythms and melodic sorcery that reverberated with the soul of the times. This segment presents the unique collaboration between Rafi's voice and Shankar-Jaikishan's musical brightness.

Extravagance Embodied: Rafi's Dynamic Articulations in Celebratory

Tunes

Rafi's joint effort with Shankar-Jaikishan saw the rise of overflowing and energetic articulations in celebratory tunes. Tunes like "Hurray! Chahe Koi Mujhe Junglee Kahe" and "Ae Phoolon Ki Rani" became songs of praise of bliss, exhibiting the irresistible enthusiasm made by the agreeable transaction of Rafi's vocals and Shankar-Jaikishan's melodic courses of action. This portion investigates the celebratory aspect of their joint effort.

Smooth Tunes: Rafi's Voice as the Heartbeat of Heartfelt Orchestras

The heartfelt orchestras made by Rafi and Shankar-Jaikishan turned into the heartbeat of a period. From the sweet "Jeene Ke Hain Chaar Noise" to the heartfelt "Ae Bhai Zara Dekh Ke Chalo," this segment digs into the resonant tunes that characterized their coordinated effort. It disentangles how Rafi's voice added layers of feeling to Shankar-Jaikishan's charming creations.

5. ### R.D. Burman's Sonic Unrest: Progressing into Contemporary Sounds

   ### Melodic Unrest: Rafi and R.D. Burman's Excursion into Contemporary Sounds

   The 1970s saw a melodic unrest, and Rafi's joint effort with R.D. Burman denoted a critical progress into contemporary sounds. This part presents the sonic upset organized by Rafi and R.D. Burman, investigating their excursion into strange melodic regions.

   ### Trial Scenes: Rafi's Versatility and R.D. Burman's Inventive Streak

   The cooperation with R.D. Burman permitted Rafi to investigate exploratory scenes that mirrored the changing elements of the music business. Melodies like "Chookar Simple Man Ko" and "Mehbooba" exhibited Rafi's flexibility to new sounds and R.D. Burman's creative streak. This section breaks down how their cooperation turned into a demonstration of the two specialists' eagerness to embrace developing melodic patterns.

6. ### Heritage and Immortal Repeats: Rafi's Voice Resounding Through Ages

Getting through Effect: Rafi's Voice as a Directing Light in Playback Singing

The getting through effect of Rafi's voice goes past wistfulness; it fills in as a directing light in the domain of playback singing. This segment investigates what Rafi's vocal ability meant for resulting ages of playback artists, molding the direction of the Indian music industry. His heritage turns into a demonstration of the immortal nature of his masterfulness.

Present day Versions and Accolades: Rafi's Presence in Contemporary Music

Contemporary specialists give recognition to Rafi through ardent interpretations and reevaluations of his ageless works of art. This portion grandstands examples of current interpretations, uncovering how Rafi's impact stays a main impetus for hopeful vocalists and a wellspring of motivation for rethinking his notorious melodies.

The getting through presence of Rafi's voice in contemporary music turns into a demonstration of the never-ending nature of his melodic heritage.

Reverberations of Time everlasting in Symphonious Solidarity

The enchanted collaboration between Mohammad Rafi's voice and immortal pieces remains as a demonstration of the everlasting excellence of music. The speculative chemistry that unfurled when Rafi loaned his voice to songs made by maestros like S.D. Burman, Shankar-Jaikishan, and R.D. Burman made a consonant solidarity that rises above the limits of time.

Rafi's voice, with its unmatched flexibility and emotive profundity, turned into the ideal instrument to convey the heap feelings epitomized in these arrangements. The cooperation with famous writers was not just a gathering of notes; it was a divine dance where every version turned into a heavenly note in the ensemble of life.

As we consider this agreeable excursion, we end up submerged in the reverberations of forever — an update that the association of a skilled voice and immortal structures has the ability to make a melodic heritage that endures everyday hardship. Mohammad Rafi's commitment to this heritage isn't simply a section in that frame of mind of playback singing; an immortal song keeps on resounding, helping us to remember the getting through wizardry that happens when a voice and tune become one.

3.3 Contributions to the cultural tapestry of mid-20th-century India

The mid-twentieth hundred years in India saw a juncture of social, social, and imaginative developments that molded the country's character. In the midst of this groundbreaking period, Mohammad Rafi arose as a melodic illuminator, making a permanent imprint on the social embroidery of the time. This investigation dives into the diverse commitments of Mohammad Rafi, looking at how his voice turned into a resounding harmony in the orchestra of mid-twentieth century India.

1. **The Socio-Social Scene of Mid-twentieth Century India**
   Setting of Progress: India During the twentieth Hundred years
   The mid-twentieth century was an essential period for India, set apart by the repercussions of freedom, the beginning of the republic, and the socio-social moves that went with these groundbreaking occasions. This segment gives a background to the period, making way for figuring out Rafi's commitments inside the unique scene of post-freedom India.
   Social Renaissance: Investigating Imaginative Thrive in Post-Freedom India
   Post-freedom India saw a social renaissance that pervaded writing, film, music, and human expression. This fragment investigates the thriving imaginative developments and the job they played in reshaping the social character of the country. It lays out the setting for understanding how Rafi's commitments turned into a necessary piece of this bigger social story.

2. **Mohammad Rafi: The Voice of a Period**
   Rafi's Excursion: From Humble Starting points to Melodic Sovereignty

Mohammad Rafi's excursion from humble starting points to turning into a melodic symbol mirrors the quintessential story of determination and ability tracking down its legitimate spot. This segment follows Rafi's initial life, the improvement of his melodic ability, and the achievements that obvious his climb to turning into the voice of a period.

Flexibility Exemplified: Rafi's Melodic Reach and Versatility

Rafi's unrivaled flexibility and versatility permitted him to cross assorted melodic kinds with equivalent artfulness. From old style interpretations to enthusiastic numbers, heartfelt songs to reflection psalms, Rafi's voice could easily catch the substance of changed feelings. This section digs into the huge melodic reach that characterized Rafi's creativity.

3. **Film Music: Rafi's Creative Material**

   The Brilliant Time of Hindi Film Music: Rafi's Featuring Job

   The mid-twentieth century is frequently alluded to as the brilliant time of Hindi film music, with writers like S.D. Burman, Shankar-Jaikishan, and R.D. Burman making tunes that turned into the heartbeat of the country. Rafi's relationship with these maestros raised film music higher than ever, making him a vital piece of the artistic renaissance. This part investigates Rafi's commitments to the brilliant time of Hindi film music.

   Ageless Soundtracks: Rafi's Effect on the Cinema

   Rafi's voice became inseparable from the wizardry of the cinema, as his interpretations revived notable characters and remarkable stories. From soul-blending love melodies to vivacious dance numbers, Rafi's effect in video form soundtracks was significant. This section looks at the persevering through tradition of Rafi's commitments to the universe of film.

4. **Impressions of Society: Rafi's Tunes as Social Mirrors**

   Social Topics in Rafi's Melodies: Reflecting the Climate

   Rafi's tunes frequently reflected the predominant social and social subjects of the time. Whether it was the festival of newly discovered opportunity, reflections on cultural issues, or the ageless investigation of affection and connections, Rafi's versions caught the outlook of mid-twentieth century India. This segment dives into the sociocultural reflections implanted in Rafi's melodies.

   Energetic Songs of devotion: Rafi's Voice To support the Country

   Rafi's commitment to energetic melodies during a time of country building was especially impactful. His versions, for example, "Kar Chale Murmur Fida" and "Yes Watan Yes Watan," became hymns that reverberated with the soul of a recently free India. This portion investigates Rafi's job in implanting energetic enthusiasm through his spirit mixing enthusiastic versions.

5. **Impact on Mainstream society: Rafi's Persevering through Presence**

   Past the Cinema: Rafi's Effect on Mainstream society

   Rafi's impact stretched out past the bounds of the entertainment world, saturating mainstream society in different structures. From radio stations to live exhibitions, his voice turned into a consistent presence in the regular daily existences of individuals. This segment investigates Rafi's effect on mainstream society and how his tunes turned into a vital piece of parties, festivities, and individual achievements.

Reflection and Ghazal Collection: Rafi's Profound Excursion Through Music

Rafi's collection reached out past the domains of film music, including reflection melodies and ghazals that displayed the otherworldly element of his masterfulness. This section investigates Rafi's otherworldly excursion through music, inspecting his interpretations that contacted the hearts of audience members on a significant level.

6. **Heritage and Proceeding with Effect: Rafi's Reverberation Through Time**

Persevering through Inheritance: Rafi's Engraving on the Melodic Legacy of India

The tradition of Mohammad Rafi perseveres as a demonstration of his unmatched commitments to the melodic legacy of India. This segment ponders the enduring effect of his masterfulness and the manners by which Rafi's melodies keep on tracking down reverberation with crowds across ages.

Accolades and Praises: Rafi's Everlasting status in Melodic Respect

Indeed, even after his passing, Rafi's inheritance lives on through ardent recognitions and tributes by specialists who perceive the persevering through effect of his commitments. This section investigates how Rafi's everlasting status is commended through melodic accolades and the manners by which contemporary craftsmen honor the maestro.

Rafi's Melodic Odyssey — An Immortal Resonation

Mohammad Rafi's commitments to the social embroidery of mid-twentieth century India are much the same as an immortal resonation that keeps on resounding through the hallways of time. His voice, with its emotive profundity and flexible reach, turned into a social milestone, reflecting the goals, delights, and difficulties of an arising country.

Rafi's effect on film music, his impression of cultural topics, and his flexible collection traversing different classes on the whole weave a story that goes past simple diversion. His melodies turned into a social mirror, mirroring the substance of a time set apart by friendly change, creative prosper, and a recently discovered feeling of character.

As we ponder Rafi's melodic odyssey, we observe that his voice isn't restricted to a particular period yet rises above worldly limits. His tunes are not simply songs; they are sections in the developing story of India — a story wherein Rafi's voice assumed a focal part in molding the social ethos of a country. Mohammad Rafi, the maestro of songs, stays a godlike symbol whose commitments reverberation through the ages, guaranteeing that his heritage is everlastingly implanted in the spirit of Indian music.

Chapter 4

Sonic Chronicle of an Era

In the huge scene of music, certain craftsmen and their manifestations become permanent imprints on the sonic material of a period. The expression "Sonic Narrative of a Period" embodies the quintessence of how music fills in as a period case, protecting and mirroring the social, social, and close to home subtleties of a particular period. This investigation dives into the multi-layered elements of sonic accounts, analyzing how music has reflected as well as effectively molded the story of particular times.

1. **Music as a Social Mirror**
   Characterizing Sonic Narratives: The Force of Music as a Period Container
   Sonic accounts, in their quintessence, are melodic stories that exemplify the soul of a specific time. They go past simple diversion, filling in as social mirrors that mirror the desires, battles, and aggregate feelings of a general public. This segment lays out the basic idea of sonic narratives and their importance in the more extensive setting of music's job in social documentation.
   The Socio-Social Embroidered artwork: How Music Reflects Society
   Music, as a powerful work of art, goes about as a mirror to cultural movements and social elements. By investigating the verses, tunes, and subjects of melodies from various periods, we can reveal the qualities, patterns, and social mentalities common during those times. This section investigates how music turns into a sonic narrative, reflecting the socio-social embroidery of its time.
2. **Development of Sonic Narratives Through Kinds**
   Kind Elements: Planning Sonic Narratives Across Melodic Styles
   Sonic narratives navigate a different range of melodic classes, each conveying its own arrangement of impacts and articulations. This segment dives into the development of sonic narratives by analyzing how different sorts, from traditional to shake, jazz to hip-jump, have added to the sonic scene of various ages.
   The Introduction of Famous Classifications: Molding Sonic Narratives in

Music History

Certain kinds have become inseparable from explicit periods, making a permanent imprint on the melodic course of events. Investigating the birth and development of famous types, for example, rock 'n' roll, punk, and electronic music gives bits of knowledge into how sonic annals are molded by the rise of earth shattering melodic developments.

3. **Maestros and Sonic Inheritances**

Unbelievable Maestros: Architecting Sonic Narratives

Behind each sonic narrative lies the virtuoso of melodic maestros — arrangers, guides, and entertainers whose masterfulness rises above time. This section investigates the commitments of unbelievable figures like Beethoven, Mozart, and other notorious arrangers who have carved their sonic inheritances on the pages of melodic history.

Sonic Trend-setters: Spearheading the Soundscapes of Periods

Past traditional domains, sonic trailblazers in famous music play played essential parts in forming the sonic narratives of their times. From Elvis Presley's stone unrest to Bounce Dylan's society fight melodies, this part features the effect of sonic trailblazers who altered melodic scenes.

4. **Mechanical Headways: Impetuses for Sonic Advancement**

The Sonic Effect of Mechanical Headways

The development of innovation has been an impetus for sonic advancement. From the gramophone to the computerized time, innovative progressions have not just altered how music is created and consumed yet have additionally impacted the sonic attributes of melodic organizations. This segment investigates how innovation goes about as a main impetus in forming sonic narratives.

Electronic Advancement: The Ascent of Computerized Soundscapes

The coming of electronic music and the computerized age introduced another time of sonic potential outcomes. Looking at the effect of synthesizers, drum machines, and computerized recording procedures on sonic scenes gives experiences into how innovation has added to the sonic annals of contemporary music.

5. **Social Developments and Sonic Reverberation**

The Dissent Melody: Sonic Narratives of Social Developments

From the beginning of time, sonic narratives have been interlaced with social and social developments. Fight melodies, specifically, act as strong sonic narratives that catch the intensity and contradiction of different developments. This section investigates the job of music in friendly activism, from the Social equality Development to against war fights.

Social Combination: Sonic Narratives in a Globalized World

In a period of globalization, sonic narratives are not generally restricted by topographical limits. The combination of different melodic customs and the rise of world music mirror the interconnectedness of societies. This part dives into how sonic narratives have developed in a globalized melodic scene.

6. **Contextual analyses: Sonic Narratives Across Many years**
The Thundering Twenties: Jazz, Gatsby, and the Sonic Freedom

The Thundering Twenties, described by jazz, the ascent of flapper culture, and the Incomparable Gatsby time, remains as an energetic part in sonic history. Looking at the sonic accounts of this period gives bits of knowledge into how music mirrored the cultural disturbances and social movements of the time.

1960s: Rock 'n' Roll, Nonconformity, and Sonic Upset

The 1960s saw a sonic upset set apart by the ascent of rock 'n' roll, the nonconformity development, and the hallucinogenic period. This contextual investigation investigates how sonic narratives of the '60s became inseparable from a feeling of defiance, social change, and melodic trial and error.

1980s: Synth-Pop, MTV, and the Sonic Feel of Overabundance

The 1980s denoted a sonic shift with the coming of synth-pop, the ascent of MTV, and the sonic style of overabundance. Dissecting the sonic narratives of the '80s discloses how music and visual components combined to make an unmistakable sonic character for the time.

2000s to Introduce: Computerized Areas, Types Impact, and Sonic Pluralism

The 21st century achieved exceptional sonic variety, with classifications impacting and sonic pluralism turning into the standard. Analyzing the sonic narratives of the 2000s to the present disentangles how innovative headways, social combination, and class obscuring have molded contemporary melodic scenes.

7. **The Persevering through Heritage: Reverberations Through Time**

Sonic Interminability: How Certain Tunes Rise above Time

A few tunes have a getting through quality that permits them to rise above transient limits. Investigating the sonic interminability of specific pieces, from old style magnum opuses to ageless pop hits, reveals insight into what compels specific sonic annals resound across ages.

The Job of Wistfulness: Sonic Accounts and Profound Memory

Wistfulness assumes a huge part in the getting through allure of sonic narratives. Looking at how certain melodies bring out close to home recollections and become ageless works of art gives experiences into the profound reverberation that music holds across time.

Sonic Narratives as Social Time Cases

The idea of "Sonic Narrative of a Time" typifies the unique transaction among music and the social, social, and mechanical scenes of unmistakable periods ever. Sonic accounts act as social time cases, safeguarding the quintessence of a period in tunes, rhythms, and verses.

Whether through the ensembles of old style maestros, the defiant songs of praise of social developments, or the trial hints of contemporary classifications, sonic accounts make a permanent imprint on the aggregate memory of humankind. As we disentangle the sonic embroidery of various times, we find that music isn't only a work of art; it is a no nonsense narrative that catches the heartbeat of humankind in each note and song.

4.1 Rafi's voice as a storyteller reflecting the highs and lows of human emotions

In the tremendous breadth of melodic history, certain voices rise above simple song, becoming expressive narrators equipped for articulating the many-sided woven artwork of human feelings. One such illuminating presence is Mohammad Rafi, whose voice fills in as a wonderful narrator, winding around stories that reverberate with the ups and downs of the human experience. This investigation dives into the creativity of Rafi's voice, analyzing the way that he turns into a story force, laying out distinctive profound scenes through his tunes.

1. **The Life systems of Rafi's Voice: A Multi-layered Instrument**
   Adaptability Represented: Rafi's Reach Across Types and Feelings
   Rafi's voice is a wonder of flexibility, equipped for navigating a broad scope of melodic types and feelings. From soul-blending heartfelt ditties to extravagant celebratory tunes, and from melancholic reflections to reflection songs, Rafi's collection exhibits a dominance over different profound ranges. This part investigates the multi-layered nature of Rafi's voice and its capacity to act as a material for a horde of human feelings.
   Specialized Splendor: Rafi's Control Over Vocal Procedures
   Past the profound reverberation, Rafi's specialized ability contributes altogether to his ability to narrate. His control over vocal strategies, including pitch regulation, apparent varieties, and immaculate control, raises his versions to a level where each note turns into a word in the story of a melody. This section digs into the specialized splendor that underlies Rafi's narrating through his voice.

2. **Love's Ensemble: Rafi's Heartfelt Stories**
   Everlasting Sentiment: Rafi's Movement of Affection's Intricacies
   One of Rafi's most convincing narrating domains is the depiction of affection in the entirety of its intricacies. From the elation of recently discovered sentiment to the piercing throb of pathetic love, Rafi's voice turns into the narrator of affection's ensemble. This part takes apart the way that Rafi's interpretations catch the subtleties of heartfelt feelings, making him an unrivaled storyteller of affection's assorted stories.
   Notorious Heartfelt Two part harmonies: Rafi's Agreeable Exchanges
   Joint efforts with female playback vocalists, especially Lata Mangeshkar, brought about immortal heartfelt two part harmonies. Melodies like "Yeh Reshmi Zulfein" and "Teri Bindiya Re" stand as demonstration of Rafi's capacity to

take part in amicable exchanges through his voice. This section investigates how these two part harmonies become melodic discussions, improving the account of adoration.

3. **Melancholic Dreams: Rafi's Depiction of Distress and Yearning**
Distress' Mourn: Rafi's Voice as a Course for Torment

Rafi's voice has an inborn capacity to explain the profundities of distress and yearning. Whether communicating the desolation of partition or the despairing of unfulfilled dreams, his versions reverberate with a significant comprehension of human torment. This part investigates how Rafi's voice turns into an impactful course for the outflow of distress.

Topical Varieties: Rafi's Portrayal of Life's Hardships

Past heartfelt distress, Rafi's voice digs into a bunch of topical varieties, describing stories of life's hardships. Melodies like "Man Re, Tu Kahe Na Dheer Dhare" from the film Chitralekha epitomize Rafi's capacity to convey the existential dilemmas and philosophical reflections that mark the human excursion. This portion investigates how Rafi's voice turns into a story string, winding through life's intricacies.

4. **Blissful Accounts: Rafi's Elevating Stories**
Festivity of Life: Rafi's Energetic Portrayals

Rafi's narrating ability reaches out to the festival of life's delights and triumphs. His voice turns into an instrument of celebration in melodies like "Aaj Mausam Bada Beimaan Hai" and "Aanewala Buddy Janewala Hai," catching the extravagance existing apart from everything else. This segment dives into how Rafi's voice turns into an upbeat storyteller, repeating the soul of festivity.

Devoted Accounts: Rafi's Voice To support the Country

Rafi's commitment to devoted tunes adds one more layer to his narrating collection. From the mixing "Kar Chale Murmur Fida" to the immortal "Yes Simple Watan Ke Logo," Rafi's voice turns into an energetic storyteller, bringing out a feeling of public pride and penance. This fragment investigates how Rafi turns into the voice of a country in snapshots of enthusiastic enthusiasm.

5. **Reflection Songs: Rafi's Otherworldly Portrayal**
Profound Excursions: Rafi's Voice as a Mode of Commitment

Rafi's narrating reaches out to the domain of otherworldliness through his interpretations of reflection psalms. Whether singing bhajans or qawwalis, his voice turns into a vessel for conveying profound otherworldly dedication. This segment digs into Rafi's capacity to describe profound excursions through his spirit mixing reflection melodies.

Interfaith Accounts: Rafi's Comprehensiveness in Profound Articulations

Rafi's voice rises above strict limits, making his reflection accounts comprehensive and widespread. Tunes like "Madhuban Mein Radhika" and "Sukh Ke Sab Saathi" feature his capacity to convey otherworldly feelings that resound across different beliefs. This fragment investigates how Rafi turns into a bringing together storyteller in the domain of otherworldliness.

6. **Rafi's Joint effort with Music Chiefs: Organizing Close to home Stories**

S.D. Burman: Heartfelt Collaboration and Melodic Stories

The coordinated effort among Rafi and music chief S.D. Burman is a great representation of deep cooperative energy, bringing about melodic stories that characterize the brilliant time of Hindi film music. This segment investigates how their organization turns into a story force, molding the close to home scenes of tunes like "Yeh Jo Mohabbat Hai" and "Clamor Dhal Jaye."

Shankar-Jaikishan: Dramatic Accounts and Ageless Songs

With Shankar-Jaikishan, Rafi participates in dramatic accounts, rejuvenating characters and stories through ageless songs. Tunes like "Jeene Ke Hain Chaar Racket" and "Yeh Raat Bheegi" become melodic stories that endure over the extreme long haul. This fragment digs into the drama of Rafi's voice under the melodic direction of Shankar-Jaikishan.

R.D. Burman: Test Accounts and Sonic Experiences

Rafi's joint effort with R.D. Burman brings about trial accounts and sonic experiences that mirror the changing soundscape of Hindi film music. Tunes like "Chura Liya Hai Tumne" and "Mehbooba" grandstand the combination of types and creative narrating through music. This part investigates how Rafi adjusts to the developing melodic accounts coordinated by R.D. Burman.

Rafi's Heritage as a Sonic Narrator

Mohammad Rafi's voice remains as an immortal demonstration of the craft of sonic narrating. His capacity to explore the range of human feelings, from adoration's delight to distress' profundities, exhibits a narrating ability that goes past simple vocalization. Rafi's voice turns into a storyteller, a minstrel whose stories resound with audience members across ages.

Rafi's heritage as a sonic narrator isn't bound to a specific type or feeling; a huge scene envelops the human involvement with all its lavishness. His accounts, woven through tunes and verses, rise above the limits of time and culture, making him an interminable voice that keeps on portraying the many-sided stories of the human heart.

As we ponder Rafi's commitment to the story of human feelings, we find that his voice stays a wellspring of comfort, happiness, and thoughtfulness. Every melody turns into a part in the book of life, and Rafi's voice, the narrator, welcomes us to submerge ourselves in the bunch feelings that characterize our reality. In the ensemble of Rafi's voice, we find the timeless reverberation of narrating through music, a heritage that reverberations through the ages.

4.2 Role in capturing the dreams, romance, and sentiments of the cinematic landscape

In the multicolored universe of Indian film, Mohammad Rafi's voice arises as an otherworldly string winding through the embroidery of dreams, sentiment, and opinions. His sonic reverberation, with its unrivaled flexibility and emotive profundity, assumed an essential part in forming the close to home scene of true to life stories. This investigation dives into the captivating domain of Rafi's commitments to the true to life scene, disentangling how his voice turned into the ethereal storyteller of dreams, the maestro of sentiment, and the caretaker of significant opinions.

1. **Dreams in Song: Rafi as the Weaver of Artistic Dreams**
   Dream Groupings and Melodic Charm
   True to life dreams frequently find their appearance in melody arrangements, and Rafi's voice was the ideal conductor for these dreamscapes. Whether it's the marvelous "Ae Phoolon Ki Rani" or the optimistic "Zindagi Ke Safar Mein," Rafi's voice adds a layer of charm, changing true to life dreams into melodic real factors. This part investigates how Rafi turned into the weaver of true to life dreams.

   Goals and Trust: Rafi's Voice as the Soundtrack of Desires
   Rafi's versions in tunes portraying characters' goals and expectations reverberate with a general appeal. His voice in tunes like "Aaj Purani Rahon Se" and "Yeh Jo Mohabbat Hai" turns into the directing power, typifying the soul of pursuing dreams. This section digs into Rafi's part in soundtracking characters' excursions toward their yearnings.

2. **Heartfelt Dream: Rafi's Voice as the Maestro of Affection**
   Deep Songs: Rafi's Heartfelt Ditties
   Rafi's voice and sentiment share an indistinguishable bond, making him the quintessential singer of adoration melodies. From the ageless "Jeene Laga Hoon" to the work of art "Chaudhvin Ka Chand Ho," Rafi's heartfelt versions inspire feelings going from the rapture of recently discovered love to the aches of division. This part investigates how Rafi's voice turns into the maestro coordinating the orchestra of affection.

   Supernatural Two part harmonies: Rafi's Agreeable Discussions of Affection
   The joint effort of Rafi with female playback artists brought about entrancing two part harmonies that stand as melodic exchanges of affection. Melodies like "Teri Bindiya Re" and "Chhup Gaye Saare Nazare" exhibit Rafi's capacity to take part in amicable discussions through his voice. This portion digs into how these two part harmonies become charming stories of sentiment.

3. **Wistful Stories: Rafi's Expressive Hug of Opinions**
   Articulations of Distress: Rafi's Voice as a Conductor for Misery
   The realistic scene frequently requires the enunciation of significant feelings, and Rafi's voice fills in as a powerful conductor for communicating distress.

His versions in tunes like "Chaudhvin Ka Chand Ho" and "Noise Dhal Jaye" become profound accounts, mirroring the profundities of human bitterness. This segment investigates how Rafi's voice embraces opinions of despairing and distress.

Philosophical Reflections: Rafi's Voice in Thoughtful Tunes

Rafi's voice takes on a scrutinizing tone in tunes that dive into philosophical reflections and contemplation. "Principal Zindagi Ka Saath Nibhata Chala Gaya" and "Zindagi Ke Safar Mein" feature Rafi's capacity to inject profundity into true to life stories through his spirit mixing interpretations. This fragment digs into how Rafi turns into the voice of examination, advancing the true to life scene with significant feelings.

4. **Rafi's Coordinated effort with Music Chiefs: Creating Artistic Feelings**

S.D. Burman: The Designer of Immortal Artistic Feelings

The coordinated effort among Rafi and S.D. Burman is a demonstration of the creating of immortal true to life feelings. Melodies like "Yeh Jo Mohabbat Hai" and "Tere Simple Sapne" epitomize how their organization turned into a thunderous power, forming the close to home scene of true to life stories. This segment investigates the emotive profundity that Rafi brought to S.D. Burman's organizations.

Shankar-Jaikishan: Sonic Speculative chemistry of Artistic Temperaments

With Shankar-Jaikishan, Rafi participated in a sonic speculative chemistry that embodied the different mind-sets of true to life stories. Tunes like "Jaane Kahan Gaye Woh Noise" and "Jeene Ki Raah" stand as instances of how their joint effort raised the close to home remainder of Hindi film music. This section investigates Rafi's job in making true to life feelings under the melodic direction of Shankar-Jaikishan.

R.D. Burman: Combination of Development and True to life Articulation

The joint effort with R.D. Burman denoted a combination of development and realistic articulation. Rafi's versions in tunes like "Aane Wala Buddy" and "Mehbooba" exhibited their capacity to try different things with sounds while keeping a profound close to home association. This part digs into how Rafi adjusted to the advancing realistic scenes organized by R.D. Burman.

5. **Rafi's Impact on Artistic Feel: Molding Close to home Stories**

Influence on Artistic Narrating: Molding Characters and Scenes

Rafi's impact on true to life narrating goes past the simple conveyance of melodies; it reaches out to forming characters and scenes. His voice turns into an indispensable piece of character advancement, adding layers of feeling and profundity to on-screen stories. This fragment investigates how Rafi's commitments rise above the melodic domain, becoming natural for true to life style.

Proceeding with Heritage: Rafi's Tunes in Contemporary Film

Indeed, even in contemporary film, Rafi's tunes keep on being embraced, remixed, and reproduced, displaying the persevering through effect of his commitments. This segment investigates how Rafi's heritage resonates in the realistic scene of today, affecting movie producers, artists, and crowds the same.

Rafi's Everlasting Reverberation in Artistic Ensemble

Mohammad Rafi's voice remains as an everlasting reverberation in the artistic ensemble, catching dreams, sentiment, and opinions with unmatched effortlessness. His capacity to mix artistic stories with emotive profundity has made a permanent imprint on the historical backdrop of Indian film music. Rafi's voice isn't simply a melodic frivolity; it is the actual heartbeat of realistic feelings.

As we think about Rafi's job in the artistic scene, we find that his voice rises above the limits of time, submerging itself in the aggregate memory of ages. Each note turns into a brushstroke, laying out clear pictures of affection, goals, distresses, and examinations on the material of celluloid. Rafi's sonic odyssey in the realistic domain stays a never-ending charm, an immortal heritage that proceeds to reverberate, and a demonstration of the significant effect of music on the profound texture of narrating in Indian film.

4.3 Invitation for listeners to immerse themselves in the golden age of Indian cinema

In the domain of music, certain voices become entries to former periods, offering audience members an immortal excursion through the social and true to life scenes of the past. Mohammad Rafi, the maestro of song, remains as an enticing aide, welcoming audience members to submerge themselves in the charming universe of the brilliant period of Indian film. This investigation unfurls the story of Rafi's suggestive greeting — a melodic stay that rises above time, welcoming audience members to rediscover the sorcery, sentiment, and energy of a period that has become inseparable from realistic greatness.

1. **The Immortal Appeal of Rafi's Voice**

   Flexibility: A Kaleidoscope of Feelings and Classifications

   Rafi's voice, with its unmatched flexibility, fills in as a sonic kaleidoscope, easily crossing a range of feelings and classes. From soul-mixing heartfelt anthems to foot-tapping dance numbers, and from strong philosophical reflections to abundant festivals of life, Rafi's collection reflects the multi-layered nature of the brilliant time of Indian film. This segment investigates how Rafi's voice turns into a general language that welcomes audience members to participate in a different cluster of feelings.

   Specialized Splendor: The Craftsmanship Behind the Song

   Past the profound profundity, Rafi's specialized brightness turns into a demonstration of the craftsmanship behind the tune. His perfect pitch control, nuanced apparent varieties, and consistent advances add to the vivid nature of his interpretations. This portion digs into the specialized complexities that hoist Rafi's voice, making it a compelling greeting for audience members to encounter melodic greatness.

2. **Heartfelt Compositions: An Excursion Through Adoration and Yearning Notable Heartfelt Two part harmonies: The Transient Enchantment of Melodic Discussions**

Rafi's joint efforts with female playback artists bring about notable heartfelt two part harmonies that embody the brilliant period of Indian film. Tunes like "Teri Bindiya Re" and "Chhup Gaye Saare Nazare" become captivating melodic discussions, welcoming audience members to remember the enchantment of true to life romantic tales. This segment investigates how these two part harmonies act as an encouragement to enjoy the immortal sentiment of bygone eras.

Awe-inspiring Songs: Rafi's Voice as the Artist of Adoration

Rafi's interpretations of heartfelt ditties unfurl like beautiful stories, communicating the heap shades of adoration — bliss, enthusiasm, and sorrow. Whether it's the profound "Chaudhvin Ka Chand Ho" or the joyous "Baharon Phool Barsao," Rafi's voice turns into the artist winding around stories of adoration. This portion welcomes audience members to submerge themselves in the melodious magnificence and profound lavishness of Rafi's heartfelt collection.

3. **Celebratory Songs of devotion: Welcoming Audience members to Move and Enjoyment**

Blissful Upliftment: Rafi's Voice in Festival of Life

The brilliant time of Indian film was set apart by upbeat festivals, and Rafi's voice filled in as the envoy of these merry minutes. Melodies like "Aaj Mausam Bada Beimaan Hai" and "Simple Samne Wali Khidki Mein" resound with the extravagance of life's celebratory minutes. This segment investigates how Rafi's voice turns into a greeting for audience members to delight in the sheer euphoria and liveliness of realistic festivals.

People Combination: Rafi's Voice in Social Festivals

Rafi's collection stretches out past the metropolitan scene, embracing the rich woven artwork of Indian society customs. Melodies like "O Simple Sona Re" and "Mera Naam Jaw Chu" meld society components with artistic energy, making a vivid encounter that transports audience members to social festivals. This portion digs into how Rafi's voice turns into an encouragement to participate in the variety of India's social mosaic.

4. **Deep Reflections: Examining Life's Significant Minutes**

Philosophical Excursions: Rafi's Voice in Thoughtful Songs

Rafi's voice takes on a thoughtful shade in melodies that dig into philosophical reflections and contemplation. "Primary Zindagi Ka Saath Nibhata Chala Gaya" and "Zindagi Ke Safar Mein" become sonic solicitations for audience members to take part in reflective excursions. This part investigates how Rafi's voice turns into an aide, welcoming audience members to consider the more profound implications of life.

Reflection Psalms: Rafi's Voice as a Way to Otherworldly Peacefulness

The brilliant age saw the formation of immortal reflection psalms, with Rafi's voice filling in as a course to otherworldly peacefulness. Whether singing bhajans or qawwalis, Rafi's versions in tunes like "Sukh Ke Sab Saathi" and "Madhuban Mein Radhika" become solicitations for audience members to set out on a profound stay. This fragment investigates how Rafi's voice turns into a passage to inward serenity.

5. **Rafi's True to life Coordinated efforts: Organization of Ageless Solicitations**

S.D. Burman's True to life Tastefulness: A Solicitation to Melodic Magnificence

The coordinated effort among Rafi and S.D. Burman is an ensemble of tastefulness, welcoming audience members to encounter melodic magnificence. Tunes like "Yeh Jo Mohabbat Hai" and "Racket Dhal Jaye" grandstand how this association turns into a persevering through greeting to delight in the immortal magnificence of artistic songs. This segment investigates the arrangement of ageless solicitations in the domain of S.D. Burman's creations.

Shankar-Jaikishan's Sonic Odyssey: Welcoming Audience members on Melodic Excursions

Under the twirly doo of Shankar-Jaikishan, Rafi's voice sets out on sonic odysseys, welcoming audience members to navigate assorted melodic scenes. Tunes like "Jeene Ke Hain Chaar Racket" and "Yeh Raat Bheegi" become solicitations for audience members to participate in the melodic excursions made by this notorious cooperation. This section investigates the changed solicitations stretched out through Shankar-Jaikishan's arrangements.

R.D. Burman's Sonic Trial and error: A Solicitation to Melodic Development

The coordinated effort with R.D. Burman makes the ways for melodic trial and error, welcoming audience members to embrace creative sounds and classifications. Melodies like "Chura Liya Hai Tumne" and "Mehbooba" become solicitations for audience members to enjoy the sonic experiences created by this powerful pair. This part investigates the modern solicitations implanted in R.D. Burman's pieces.

6. **The Getting through Inheritance: Rafi's Solicitations Resounding Across Time**

Contemporary Repeats: Rafi's Melodies in the Cutting edge Period

Mohammad Rafi's heritage stretches out past the brilliant age, with his tunes proceeding to track down reverberation in the contemporary period. Whether through remixes, entertainments, or accolades, Rafi's solicitations to melodic wistfulness reverberation across time, welcoming new ages to find the enchantment of his immortal songs. This part investigates how Rafi's voice stays a perpetual greeting, rising above generational limits.

Social Embroidery: Rafi's Voice as a Scaffold Between Periods

Rafi's voice turns into a scaffold that interfaces various periods, welcoming audience members to cross the social embroidery of Indian film. His tunes act as solicitations to investigate the developing elements of narrating, music, and cultural changes. This fragment dives into how Rafi's voice turns into a social continuum, welcoming audience members to interface with the rich legacy of Indian film.

The Never-ending Greeting to Euphonic Sentimentality

Mohammad Rafi's voice stretches out a never-ending greeting to euphonic wistfulness, enticing audience members to cross the brilliant time of Indian film. His voice isn't simply an assortment of songs; a vivid encounter rises above transient limits. Rafi's solicitations, woven through heartfelt songs, celebratory hymns, profound reflections, and realistic joint efforts, stand as ageless reverberations, welcoming audience members to savor the sorcery of bygone eras.

As we acknowledge Rafi's greeting and submerge ourselves in the brilliant period of Indian film, we find tunes as well as minutes frozen in time, embodying the embodiment of a period that keeps on enamoring hearts. Rafi's voice, with its immortal charm, welcomes us to be essential for a melodic excursion — one that rises above the conventional and embraces the exceptional. In the ensemble of Rafi's songs, we track down a timeless greeting to delight in the excellence, sentimentality, and social extravagance of a period that will everlastingly stay brilliant in the chronicles of Indian artistic history.

Chapter 5

Enduring Artistry

In the immense span of human imagination, there exists a select classification of works that rises above the limits of time, making a permanent imprint on the social embroidery of mankind. This domain of persevering through imaginativeness includes show-stoppers that endure everyday hardship, resounding across ages and holding their significance. This investigation dives into the complex idea of persevering through imaginativeness, analyzing its substance, disentangling its indications across different teaches, and testing the variables that lift specific manifestations to the echelons of agelessness.

1. **Characterizing Persevering through Imaginativeness: The Speculative chemistry of Immortal Manifestations**
1. **Immortality as a Measure:**
   Persevering through masterfulness is set apart by its capacity to endure for the long haul, rising above the transient imperatives that keep numerous innovative undertakings. It is a combination of all inclusive allure, social importance, and enduring effect. Works that have these traits become more than simple antiques; they become vessels conveying the aggregate feelings, considerations, and yearnings of humankind across ages.
2. **Qualities of Getting through Craftsmanship:**

To distil the substance of getting through imaginativeness, one should examine its qualities. Development, profundity, and profound reverberation arise as normal qualities that tight spot these manifestations together. The speculative chemistry of these components changes a piece of craftsmanship into an immortal element, equipped for getting significant reactions from crowds no matter what the period.

II. The Orchestra of Visual Expressions: Artworks, Models, and Immortal Feel

1. **Compositions: Representations of Immortality:**
   The material turns into an entrance to time everlasting in the realm of persevering through imaginativeness. Notorious canvases have the ability to rise above time, catching feelings and stories that resound across ages. Show-stoppers like Leonardo da Vinci's "Mona Lisa" and Vincent van Gogh's "Brilliant Evening" exemplify the capacity of visual workmanship to scratch itself into the aggregate memory of humankind.
2. **Figures: Cutting Everlasting status in Stone:**

In the domain of figure, getting through masterfulness takes on a three-layered structure. Models, whether etched from marble or cast in bronze, can summon feelings that endure the attacks of time. Michelangelo's "David" and Auguste Rodin's "The Scholar" act as demonstrations of the persevering through nature of sculptural show-stoppers.

III. Writing: The Composed Woven artwork of Getting through Stories

1. **Exemplary Books: Scholarly Mainstays of Agelessness:**
   The composed word turns into an unfading vessel for getting through stories. Exemplary books, through their nuanced narrating and investigation of the human condition, achieve an immortal quality. Works, for example, Leo Tolstoy's "War and Harmony" and Jane Austen's "Pride and Bias" keep on charming perusers, offering experiences into the intricacies of life that rise above fleeting limits.
2. **Immortal Sonnets: Sections Reverberating Through Ages:**

Verse, with its expressive quickness, has a special ability to typify significant opinions. Getting through sonnets, like William Wordsworth's "Daffodils" and Emily Dickinson's "Since I was unable to stop for Death," resound across time, winding around sections that reverberation through the ages and proceed to move and bring out feelings in each peruser.

IV. The Harmonies of Getting through Tunes: Music Past the Ages

1. **Traditional Structures: Reverberations of Time everlasting:**
   In the domain of music, persevering through masterfulness tracks down articulation in old style structures. These immortal tunes, frequently created hundreds of years prior, keep on enchanting crowds with their unpredictable harmonies and close to home profundity. Crafted by maestros like Mozart, Beethoven, and Bach rise above the constraints of their periods, making an orchestra that reverberations through the hallways of time.
2. **Notorious Melodies: The Soundtrack of Aggregate Memory:**

Past old style arrangements, persevering through masterfulness in music stretches out to notable melodies that become the soundtrack of aggregate memory. Whether it's Blunt Sinatra's "My Way" or The Beatles' "Hello Jude," these tunes catch the outlook of their time and keep on bringing out feelings, becoming hymns that reverberate across ages.

V. Performing Expressions: Dance and Theater as Living Confirmations

1. **Dance: Arranging Immortal Developments:**
   In the domain of dance, persevering through masterfulness is scratched in the ease of developments and the declaration of feelings through the actual structure. Dance sytheses, for example, those by Martha Graham or traditional Indian dance structures like Bharatanatyam, typify the substance of persevering through masterfulness, enamoring crowds and rising above social and transient obstructions.

2. **Theater: The Everlasting Phase of Human Show:**

Theater, as a living and breathing fine art, is a demonstration of getting through stories established on the stage. Plays by Shakespeare, similar to "Hamlet" and "Romeo and Juliet," keep on being performed around the world, representing the immortal subjects and characters that reverberate with crowds independent of the age.

VI. Realistic Immortality: Casings Frozen in Forever

1. **Exemplary Movies: Celluloid Accounts of Time:**
   The wizardry of persevering through creativity reaches out to the universe of film. Exemplary movies, through their narrating, cinematography, and exhibitions, become celluloid narratives that endure for the long haul. Works like "Gone with the Breeze" and "Casablanca" are not simply films; they are social antiquities that keep on enthralling crowds a very long time after their delivery.

2. **Ageless Chiefs: Visionaries Forming Artistic Inheritances:**

Behind the focal point, getting through imaginativeness is in many cases encapsulated by visionary chiefs whose realistic language rises above ages. Producers like Alfred Hitchcock and Akira Kurosawa created stories that were not bound to their contemporary milieu yet rather addressed general subjects, guaranteeing their spot in the pantheon of persevering through true to life creativity.

VII. Factors Forming Getting through Creativity: From Social Reverberation to Imaginative Respectability

1. **Social Reverberation:**
   Works of getting through imaginativeness frequently have a widespread quality that rises above social contrasts. They tap into the common human experience,

reverberating with people across assorted foundations. This social reverberation guarantees that the craftsmanship stays important and significant, regardless of the cultural setting where it was made.

2. **Creative Uprightness:**

The uprightness of the craftsman and their obligation to their specialty assume a crucial part in making persevering through works. Craftsmen who inject their manifestations with realness, enthusiasm, and a certified association with the topic add to the enduring effect of their specialty. The truthfulness of articulation turns into a signal that directs the work through the flows of time.

VIII. Protection and Heritage: Supporting Persevering through Workmanship for People in the future

1. **Protection Endeavors:**
   Protecting getting through craftsmanship requires committed preservation endeavors. Whether it's reestablishing works of art, digitizing writing, or remastering exemplary movies, these undertakings guarantee that the workmanship stays available and holds its unique pith for people in the future.
2. **Instructive Drives:**

Instructive projects and drives assume an essential part in sending the appreciation for getting through masterfulness. By incorporating these works into educational plans, foundations develop a comprehension of the social, verifiable, and imaginative meaning of these manifestations, cultivating an adoration for immortal magnum opuses.

The Persevering through Ensemble of Human Imagination

Taking everything into account, persevering through imaginativeness is the ensemble of human innovativeness that resounds through time, winding around together the strings of visual expressions, writing, music, performing expressions, film, and then some. These immortal manifestations act as windows into the aggregate soul of mankind, offering bits of knowledge, inciting feelings, and interfacing people across ages.

The speculative chemistry of persevering through masterfulness lies in its capacity to rise above the limits of its creation, turning into a living demonstration of the human soul's unfathomable limit with respect to articulation. As we explore the flows of time, we track down comfort, motivation, and a feeling of coherence in the persevering through works that have endured the ages.

It is through these works of art that the reverberation of past voices resounds with our own, and the material of time turns into a common space where the brushstrokes of innumerable specialists, scholars, performers, and makers keep on forming the embroidery of our aggregate presence. Persevering through creativity isn't just an assortment of manifestations; the timeless ensemble goes with us on our excursion through the steadily changing scenes of human experience.

5.1 Recognition of the album as a testament to Rafi's enduring musical brilliance

In the domain of Indian music, barely any voices have accomplished the agelessness and comprehensiveness that Mohammad Rafi's voice orders. His commitments to the Indian entertainment world have made a permanent imprint, and one striking demonstration of his getting through melodic splendor is embodied in the acknowledgment of a gathering collection that fills in as an organized excursion through his tremendous and different collection. This investigation digs into the significant acknowledgment presented to such a collection, inspecting how it remains as a demonstration of Rafi's getting through melodic brightness, crossing types, feelings, and many years.

1. **Setting the Stage: The Verifiable and Melodic Scene of Mohammad Rafi's Profession**
1. **The Brilliant Period of Hindi Film:**
   Mohammad Rafi's profession unfurled during what is frequently alluded to as the "Brilliant Time" of Hindi film, a period set apart by the making of immortal works of art and the intermingling of unbelievable writers, lyricists, and playback vocalists. This time established the groundwork for Rafi's melodic excursion, permitting his voice to become inseparable from the feelings and stories of the cinema.
2. **Different Types, Endless Feelings:**

Rafi's flexibility as a playback vocalist is unrivaled. From soul-blending heartfelt anthems to foot-tapping dance numbers, philosophical reflections to reflection songs, his voice consistently navigated assorted kinds and caught the embodiment of bunch feelings. This multi-layered capacity turned into a sign of his getting through melodic splendor.

II. The Introduction of a Gathering Collection: Organizing Rafi's Immortal Tunes

1. **Perceiving the Melodic Heritage:**
   The choice to order a devoted collection highlighting Mohammad Rafi's hits is, in itself, an acknowledgment of the unmatched melodic heritage he abandoned. It recognizes the persevering through allure of his tunes and looks to organize an assortment that fills in as an exhaustive recognition for his commitments to the Indian music industry.
2. **Exploring Many years: Sequential or Topical Course of action:**

Gathering Rafi's melodies requires choices on the best way to organize them. A few collections pick an ordered excursion through his profession, permitting audience members to observe the development of his style. Others might adopt a topical strategy, gathering tunes in light of feelings, temperaments, or classifications.

The two methodologies add to the acknowledgment of Rafi's flexibility and the advancement of his melodic ability over the long haul.

III. Investigating the Aggregation: An Odyssey Through Rafi's Differed Collection

1. **Heartfelt Dreams: The Profound Songs:**
   One can't navigate the melodic scene of Mohammad Rafi without being submerged in the profound anthems that characterize his heartfelt collection. Melodies like "Chaudhvin Ka Chand Ho" and "Jeene Laga Hoon" exemplify the substance of affection, displaying Rafi's capacity to pass the most significant feelings on through his smooth voice.

2. **Foot-Tapping Works of art: The Vigorous Rhythms:**
   Rafi's flexibility stretches out past the domain of piercing tunes. His voice easily changes to peppy and fiery rhythms, making foot-tapping works of art that stay carved in the recollections of audience members. Whether it's the energetic "Aaj Mausam Bada Beimaan Hai" or the abundant "Yippee! Chahe Koi Mujhe Jun-glee Kahe," Rafi's energy implants these melodies with an irresistible liveliness.

3. **Philosophical Reflections: Exploring the Profundities of Thought:**

Rafi's voice turns into a conductor for significant philosophical appearance in melodies that investigate the more profound implications of life and presence. "Principal Zindagi Ka Saath Nibhata Chala Gaya" and "Zindagi Ke Safar Mein" exhibit his capacity to mix examination and thoughtfulness into melodic accounts, lifting these organizations to immortal reflections on the human experience.

IV. Acknowledgment in Grants and Awards: Regarding Rafi's Creative Dominance

1. **Public and Global Acknowledgment:**
   The gathering collection, as a demonstration of Rafi's getting through melodic brightness, frequently lines up with the various honors and awards he got during his renowned lifetime. From Public Film Grants to worldwide distinctions, Rafi's commitments were commended on different stages, supporting the acknowledgment of his masterfulness on a worldwide scale.

2. **Lifetime Accomplishment Praises: After death Festivities:**

Rafi's impact reaches out past his lifespan, and post mortem awards, for example, lifetime accomplishment praises keep on recognizing the enduring effect of his melodic inheritance. These distinctions add to the acknowledgment of Rafi's persevering through brightness, stressing the never-ending reverberation of his commitments to the universe of music.

V. The Persevering through Allure: An Immortal Association with Crowds

1. **Generational Coherence:**
   The acknowledgment of a gathering collection as a demonstration of Rafi's persevering through melodic splendor is entwined with its capacity to keep an immortal association with crowds across ages. Rafi's tunes have the special nature of resounding with audience members independent of the period they have a place with, making a scaffold that traverses many years and guarantees the coherence of his melodic heritage.

2. **Contemporary Reverberation:**

Indeed, even in the contemporary music scene, Rafi's tunes track down reverberation. Whether through reevaluations, remixes, or recognitions by advanced specialists, the getting through allure of his structures perseveres. This contemporary reverberation further cements the acknowledgment of Rafi's melodic brightness, delineating how his imaginativeness rises above the limits of time.

VI. Inheritance Past Limits: Rafi's Worldwide Effect

1. **Culturally diverse Impact:**
   Acknowledgment of the collection reaches out past public lines, featuring Rafi's diverse effect. His melodies have been embraced by crowds worldwide, finding a spot in the hearts of audience members who may not grasp the language however interface with the widespread feelings passed on through his voice. This worldwide acknowledgment turns into a demonstration of the global meaning of Rafi's persevering through melodic brightness.

2. **Coordinated efforts and Social Trades:**

Rafi's coordinated efforts with worldwide specialists and his melodies' consideration in worldwide undertakings highlight the acknowledgment of his imaginativeness on a global stage. Social trades worked with by his music add to encouraging a common appreciation for the rich melodic legacy he abandoned, rising above geological limits.

The Never-ending Reverberations of Rafi's Tunes

The acknowledgment of a gathering collection as a demonstration of Mohammad Rafi's getting through melodic brightness is a festival of a craftsman whose effect rises above time. Through soul-blending numbers, foot-tapping works of art, and philosophical reflections, Rafi's voice turns into an immortal reverberation, resounding as the decades progressed and interfacing with the hearts of audience members across the globe.

The gathering collection fills in as an organized excursion through Rafi's fluctuated collection, offering a brief look into the complex idea of his creativity. Grants, honors, and global acknowledgment further approve the persevering through allure of Rafi's music, guaranteeing that his heritage stays alive in the hearts of ages on the way. As the tunes of Mohammad Rafi keep on winding around their sorcery, the acknowledgment presented to his melodic splendor remains as a never-ending recognition for a his immortal craftsman, through his immortal manifestations, has turned into an undying presence in the realm of music.

5.2 Reflection on the timeless nature of Rafi's voice and its impact on listeners

In the kaleidoscope of melodic history, certain voices arise as immortal, rising above the limits of time and class. Mohammad Rafi, an illuminating presence in the domain of playback singing, remains as an embodiment of such everlasting reverberation. This reflection sets out on an excursion through the ethereal nature of Rafi's voice, looking at its immortal nature and the significant effect it has had on audience members across ages. From the spirit mixing melodies to the extravagant hymns, Rafi's voice turns into a conductor for feelings that reverberation through time.

1. **The Confounding Quintessence of Rafi's Voice**

1. **A Voice Past Time:**
   Rafi's voice has a confounding quality that resists the requirements of worldly limits. It isn't just a sound however a living element that keeps on reviving tunes across many years. The immaculateness, flexibility, and emotive profundity of his voice add to its immortal charm, making it an interminable wellspring of comfort and satisfaction for audience members.

2. **Flexibility as a Mark:**

   Rafi's flexibility turns into a mark of his immortal allure. From the tragic despairing of a heartfelt song to the rich festival of life in a lively number, his voice easily navigates different classifications. This versatility guarantees that his effect isn't bound to a particular close to home or melodic domain yet reaches out to the whole range of human experience.

II. The Profound Reverberation: An Ensemble of Human Sentiments

1. **Heartfelt Dreams:**
   In the domain of heartfelt melodies, Rafi's voice turns into a vessel for the most significant articulations of adoration. Tunes like "Chaudhvin Ka Chand Ho" and "Tum Jo Mil Gaye Ho" typify the substance of sentiment, and Rafi's interpretation changes these pieces into immortal articulations of the heart.
   The profound reverberation is to such an extent that audience members, no matter what their own heartfelt encounters, wind up brought into the reminiscent account woven by Rafi's voice.

2. **Blissful Upliftment:**
Rafi's voice isn't restricted to the profundities of despairing; it ascends with equivalent brightness to commend the delights of life. Tunes like "Aaj Mausam Bada Beimaan Hai" and "Yeh Jo Mohabbat Hai" become hymns of delight, their irresistible enthusiasm reverberating with audience members and inspiring spirits across ages. Rafi's capacity to imbue richness into his interpretations concretes his place as a maestro fit for bringing out a range of feelings.

3. **Philosophical Examinations:**

Past the domains of affection and festivity, Rafi's voice turns into a course for philosophical reflections. Tunes like "Principal Zindagi Ka Saath Nibhata Chala Gaya" and "Zindagi Ke Safar Mein" dive into the significant inquiries of presence, and Rafi's delivering changes these sytheses into reflections on life's excursion. His voice turns into an aide, welcoming audience members to mull over the more profound implications of their own encounters.

III. The Effect on Close to home Therapy: Recuperating Through Rafi's Songs

1. **Soothing Force of Music:**
Music, at its pith, has a soothing power that rises above simple diversion. Rafi's voice, with its emotive wealth, turns into a restorative instrument for audience members exploring the intricacies of life. Whether in snapshots of satisfaction, grievousness, or consideration, his tunes act as buddies that comprehend, reverberate, and give comfort.

2. **Exploring Sadness and Misfortune:**
In the midst of sadness and misfortune, Rafi's voice turns into a consoling presence. His interpretations of melodies like "Chalo Dildar Chalo" and "Tum Jo Mil Gaye Ho" can comfort, offering an ointment to injured hearts. The significant sympathy implanted in his voice makes a space for audience members to lament, recuperate, and track down comfort in the immortal songs.

3. **A Soundtrack to Life's Achievements:**

Rafi's voice becomes entwined with the individual stories of audience members, filling in as a soundtrack to life's achievements. Whether it's a wedding, a festival, or a tranquil snapshot of reflection, his tunes become the scenery to these minutes. The effect isn't simply hear-able; a profound close to home association rises above the actual demonstration of tuning in.

IV. The Masterfulness in Rafi's Vocal Procedure

1. **Specialized Brightness:**
Rafi's persevering through influence isn't exclusively credited to the profound profundity of his voice; his specialized brightness assumes a significant part. His

flawless pitch control, nuanced apparent varieties, and consistent advances add to the vivid nature of his interpretations. This specialized ability hoists Rafi from a simple playback vocalist to a virtuoso whose control over the medium turns into a fundamental piece of his persevering through inheritance.

2. **Expressive Subtleties:**

The nuances and subtleties in Rafi's voice uncover a craftsman profoundly receptive to the expressive capability of each and every note. Whether it's a delicate vibrato in a heartfelt song or a strong crescendo in a high-energy piece, Rafi's voice turns into an instrument of unmatched expressiveness. These subtleties add layers of significance to the verses, making a multi-layered sonic experience.

V. Heritage Through Coordinated efforts: The Speculative chemistry of Rafi's Voice with Music Chiefs

1. **Notable Joint efforts:**
   Rafi's inheritance reaches out past his singular splendor; it is additionally profoundly entwined with his joint efforts with amazing music chiefs. The speculative chemistry made when Rafi's voice meets the sytheses of maestros like S.D. Burman, Shankar-Jaikishan, and R.D. Burman brings about ageless manifestations. Every joint effort turns into a section in the story of Rafi's getting through influence, displaying the collaboration between his voice and the melodic virtuoso of these maestros.

2. **Versatility Across Kinds:**

The variety of Rafi's joint efforts highlights his versatility across kinds. From the old style complexities of S.D. Burman's organizations to the exploratory hints of R.D. Burman, Rafi's voice consistently explores assorted melodic scenes. This flexibility guarantees that his effect isn't restricted to a particular period or melodic style yet reverberates across the consistently developing soundscape of Indian music.

VI. The Immortal Quality in Social Setting: Rafi's Voice as a Social Legacy

1. **Social Symbol:**
   Rafi's voice rises above individual imaginativeness; it turns into a social symbol that mirrors the ethos of a period. His tunes encapsulate post-freedom India, mirroring the hopefulness, sentiment, and yearnings of the time. Rafi's voice turns into a sonic case that typifies the social subtleties of a former period, permitting audience members to navigate the socio-social scene through the crystal of his songs.

2. **Generational Handover: Passing the Melodic Mallet:**

The immortal idea of Rafi's voice is clear in its capacity to pass consistently starting with one age then onto the next. The tunes that resounded with audience members during the 1960s keep on enamoring the hearts of new ages. This generational handover isn't simply a demonstration of Rafi's getting through influence yet in addition an impression of the comprehensiveness of his voice, which rises above generational partitions.

VII. The Advanced Age: Rafi's Voice in the Cutting edge Mechanical Scene

1. **Computerized Resurgence:**
   In the computerized age, Rafi's voice encounters a resurgence through web-based stages and real time features. The openness of his melodies to a worldwide crowd guarantees that his effect reaches out a long ways past the limits of geology. The computerized scene turns into a channel for acquainting Rafi's immortal tunes with new audience members, guaranteeing the ceaselessness of his heritage in a steadily developing mechanical scene.

2. **Remix Culture and Discussions:**

The advanced age likewise brings difficulties, especially as remixes and reevaluations. While some view these as a festival of Rafi's heritage, others contend that they weaken the genuineness of the first creations. The debates encompassing remixes highlight the defensive opinion audience members harbor for the holiness of Rafi's voice and the immortal quality it addresses.

VIII. The Intergenerational Allure: An Extension Between Times

1. **Rediscovery by New Ages:**
   Rafi's voice goes through a never-ending course of rediscovery by new ages. Youthful audience members, presented to his tunes through different mediums, frequently end up enamored by the immortal nature of his voice. The comprehensiveness of feelings conveyed in Rafi's melodies turns into a scaffold that associates audience members across different age gatherings, laying out a feeling of progression in the enthusiasm for his masterfulness.

2. **Instructive Worth: Protecting Melodic Legacy:**

Rafi's voice likewise holds instructive worth, filling in as a window into the development of Indian music. Instructive foundations perceive the meaning of concentrating on his versions to comprehend the subtleties of playback singing, vocal method, and the social setting implanted in his tunes. This instructive aspect guarantees that Rafi's voice turns into a piece of educational plans, adding to the protection of melodic legacy.

IX. Difficulties to Immortality: Copyright Issues and Commercialization

1. **Copyright Difficulties:**
   The protection of Rafi's immortal songs faces difficulties as copyright issues. Legitimate intricacies encompassing the responsibility for organizations have, on occasion, ruined the consistent accessibility of his melodies on different stages. These difficulties highlight the sensitive harmony between business interests and the safeguarding of social legacy.
2. **Commercialization of Inheritance:**

The commercialization of Rafi's inheritance, through stock, accolade shows, and supports, brings up issues about the validness of saving his immortal nature. While these undertakings add to keeping his name alive, they likewise represent the gamble of decreasing his creative commitments to simple items. Finding some kind of harmony between business suitability and protecting the veritable substance of Rafi's heritage becomes essential in guaranteeing the respectability of his ageless effect.

The Unfading Reverberations of Rafi's Voice

The reflection on the immortal idea of Mohammad Rafi's voice and its effect on audience members rises above the limits of a simple hear-able experience. Rafi's voice turns into a living substance, resounding with the most profound openings of human feelings and winding around a multifaceted embroidery of immortal tunes. From the heartfelt songs that mix the heart to the philosophical reflections that immediate thoughtfulness, Rafi's voice is a vessel for the whole range of human experience.

The persevering through effect of Rafi's voice lies in its close to home reverberation as well as in its versatility across types, its cooperative energy with unbelievable music chiefs, and its capacity to turn into a social symbol. In the computerized age, Rafi's voice tracks down new life, acquainting itself with progressive ages and laying out an intergenerational span that associates audience members across time.Difficulties, for example, copyright issues and commercialization highlight the delicacy of safeguarding agelessness in a steadily developing social scene. In any case, the certified love and respect audience members harbor for Rafi's voice, as well as instructive drives that mean to pass on his melodic heritage, stand as watchmen against weakening the credibility of his effect.As we keep on exploring the flows of time, Mohammad Rafi's voice stays an unfading reverberation, an everlasting song that rises above the limitations of the fleeting. Its effect on audience members isn't restricted to a particular period or segment however resonates across ages, making it a demonstration of the getting through nature of creative brightness and the immortal force of music to interface the human spirit across the tremendous breadth of time.

5.3 The album as a tribute to the legacy of Mohammad Rafi in the world of music

In the orchestra of Indian playback singing, the name Mohammad Rafi remains as an unmatched maestro whose voice keeps on reverberating through the hallways of time. One significant demonstration of his persevering through heritage is found in the production of a collection fastidiously organized as a recognition. This investigation digs into the complexities of the collection, taking apart its job as a respectful tribute and a demonstration of the never-ending effect of Mohammad Rafi on the universe of music.

1. **Setting the Stage: Rafi's Persevering through Heritage in the Melodic Domain**
1. **The Maestro's Excursion:**
   Mohammad Rafi's excursion in the realm of music follows a direction that lines up with the development of Indian film. From the brilliant time of Hindi film to the contemporary scene, Rafi's voice has been a steady friend for crowds, improving the realistic involvement in its unrivaled profundity and flexibility.
2. **Disentangling the Flexibility:**

Rafi's heritage is scratched in the unmatched flexibility of his voice. His capacity to flawlessly change from soul-mixing numbers to lively songs of devotion and from traditional interpretations to exploratory structures hardens his situation as a maestro whose impact ranges across classes. The collection, as a recognition, looks to catch and commend this multi-layered part of Rafi's melodic virtuoso.

II. Creating a Recognition Collection: The Specialty of Curation

1. **The Substance of Curation:**
   The production of a collection devoted to Mohammad Rafi is a shrewd cycle that includes fastidious curation. The test lies in choosing the most notable versions as well as in winding around them together in a story that gives recognition to the different features of Rafi's masterfulness. The collection turns into a material where each track is a brushstroke, adding to the general representation of a melodic legend.
2. **Exploring Through Many years: Sequence or Topics:**

Curation choices assume a vital part in molding the recognition collection. Would it be a good idea for it to follow an ordered grouping, permitting audience members to travel through the development of Rafi's style? On the other hand, would it be a good idea for it to take on a topical methodology, gathering melodies in light of feelings, states of mind, or classes? The two methodologies are loaded down with importance, adding to the general story that unfurls as a recognition for Rafi's melodic inheritance.

III. Melodic Odyssey: Investigating the Profundities of Rafi's Collection

1. **Reverberations of Sentiment:**
   Rafi's voice turns into an exemplification of sentiment in the domain of playback singing. The accolade collection explores through the spirit blending songs

that characterize his heartfelt collection. Tracks like "Chaudhvin Ka Chand Ho" and "Tum Jo Mil Gaye Ho" become strong tokens of Rafi's capacity to pass the most significant feelings of adoration on through the creativity of his voice.

2. **Foot-Tapping Delight:**

The collection doesn't only wait in the melancholic notes of sentiment; it wanders into the extravagant songs of praise that describe Rafi's more celebratory versions. Whether it's the fun loving nature of "Aaj Mausam Bada Beimaan Hai" or the liveliness of "Yippee! Chahe Koi Mujhe Junglee Kahe," the collection embodies the irresistible enthusiasm that Rafi injected into his cheerful pieces.

3. **Philosophical Insights:**

Past sentiment and festivity, Rafi's voice dives into the philosophical domains of music. The collection turns into a vessel for melodies like "Fundamental Zindagi Ka Saath Nibhata Chala Gaya" and "Zindagi Ke Safar Mein," where Rafi's voice changes into a savvy, conferring immortal insight and reflections on life's excursion.

IV. Regarding Creative Authority: Rafi's Effect on the Melodic Scene

1. **Grants and Honors: A Melodic Laureate:**

The recognition collection conforms to the various honors and awards presented to Rafi during his distinguished lifetime. From Public Film Grants to global distinctions, Rafi's commitments were commended on different stages, highlighting his status as a melodic laureate. The collection, as a recognition, turns into a vehicle for conveying the significant effect of Rafi's creative dominance.

2. **Lifetime Accomplishment: Post mortem Festivities:**

Rafi's impact reaches out past his lifespan, with after death awards, for example, lifetime accomplishment praises proceeding to recognize the enduring effect of his melodic inheritance. These distinctions add to the acknowledgment of Rafi's persevering through splendor, underlining the never-ending reverberation of his commitments to the universe of music.

V. The Advancing Soundscape: Rafi's Importance in Contemporary Music

1. **Immortal Reverberation:**

The recognition collection fills in as an extension between periods, featuring Rafi's immortal reverberation. While established in the soundscape of the past, his voice tracks down importance in the contemporary melodic scene. Whether through reevaluations, covers, or recognitions by advanced craftsmen, the collection features how Rafi's imaginativeness rises above worldly limits.

2. **Remix Discussions: Exploring Imaginative Respectability:**

The advancement of Rafi's music likewise experiences difficulties, especially as remixes and reevaluations. The accolade collection, while observing Rafi's heritage, explores the fragile harmony between giving proper respect and keeping up with the realness of the first organizations. The debates encompassing remixes highlight the defensive opinion audience members harbor for the sacredness of Rafi's voice.

VI. Worldwide Resonations: Rafi's Voice Past Boundaries

1. **Multifaceted Impact:**
   The accolade collection recognizes the worldwide effect of Rafi's voice, reverberating with crowds past Indian boundaries. His tunes have been embraced by audience members around the world, rising above etymological boundaries to associate with the general feelings passed on through his voice. The collection turns into a demonstration of Rafi's multifaceted impact and his situation as a worldwide melodic symbol.

2. **Coordinated efforts with Worldwide Specialists:**

Rafi's coordinated efforts with worldwide craftsmen further upgrade his worldwide melodic impression. The recognition collection might include examples where Rafi's voice amicably converges with different melodic customs, making a combination that rises above social limits. These coordinated efforts add to the collection's story of Rafi's widespread allure.

VII. Instructive Importance: Safeguarding Rafi's Melodic Teaching method

1. **Academic Worth:**
   The recognition collection isn't just a festival yet in addition holds instructive worth. It turns into a storehouse of Rafi's melodic teaching method, offering an organized determination that fills in as a learning asset for trying vocalists, music lovers, and researchers. Instructive drives perceive the meaning of concentrating on Rafi's versions to comprehend the subtleties of playback singing, vocal procedure, and the social setting implanted in his tunes.

2. **Sustaining Melodic Legacy:**

By safeguarding Rafi's melodic legacy, the accolade collection adds to the propagation of Indian melodic customs. The collection, in its job as an instructive device, guarantees that Rafi's commitments stay important across ages, cultivating a comprehension of the social, verifiable, and imaginative meaning of his work.

VIII. Challenges and Moral Contemplations: Exploring the Inheritance

1. **Copyright Difficulties:**
   The formation of a recognition collection faces difficulties, especially in the domain of copyright issues. Lawful intricacies encompassing the responsibility

for creations can influence the consistent accessibility of Rafi's tunes on different stages. Exploring these difficulties becomes vital in safeguarding the honesty of the recognition collection and Rafi's melodic heritage.

2. **Commercialization Concerns:**

While business practicality is inborn in the development of a recognition collection, moral contemplations should be vital. The sensitive harmony between business achievement and saving the certified quintessence of Rafi's heritage turns into a tightrope walk. Wandering excessively far into commercialization represents the gamble of diminishing his creative commitments to simple wares.

A Melodic Tribute to an Eternal Inheritance

The collection created as a recognition for Mohammad Rafi arises as a melodic respect to an undying heritage. Through cautious curation, the collection winds around a story that rises above the fleeting, catching the embodiment of Rafi's multi-layered masterfulness. It honors the heartfelt songs, the blissful hymns, and the philosophical insights that characterize his melodic collection.

The collection's importance stretches out past a simple gathering; a sonic embroidery mirrors Rafi's effect on the melodic scene, his persevering through pertinence, and the general allure of his voice. As it explores through the difficulties of remix discussions, worldwide resonances, and instructive objectives, the collection remains as a watchman of Rafi's inheritance, protecting it for current and people in the future.

In the immense orchestra of Indian playback singing, the collection turns into an extraordinary development, resounding with the reverberations of Rafi's voice that keep on resonating across time. It is a demonstration of the getting through force of music to associate hearts, rise above limits, and deify the commitments of a maestro like Mohammad Rafi in the realm of music.

Chapter 6

Conclusion

As we navigate the tunes and subtleties of Mohammad Rafi's renowned lifetime, we end up at the finishing up crescendo — a musical conclusion to an excursion that has traversed many years, rose above limits, and made a permanent imprint on the chronicles of Indian music. The end to this investigation of Rafi's inheritance isn't simply an endpoint; it is a reflection on the getting through reverberation of his voice, the immortal effect on audience members, and the multi-layered components of his melodic odyssey.

1. **The Ageless Reverberation: Rafi's Inheritance Across Periods**
1. **Eternality in Songs:**
   Mohammad Rafi's inheritance isn't restricted to the sequential markers of birth and passing. All things being equal, it exists in the eternality of his tunes, the evergreen idea of his melodies that challenge the limits of time. As we close this excursion, it is basic to recognize that Rafi's voice isn't a remnant of the past yet a timeless reverberation that keeps on resounding with audience members across ages.
2. **Generational Progression:**

One of the striking parts of Rafi's inheritance is its consistent change across ages. His tunes, which resounded through the passages of the twentieth 100 years, track down a restored crowd in the 21st. The capacity of Rafi's voice to interface with contemporary audience members is a demonstration of its immortal quality, laying out a scaffold that rises above the transient holes between periods.

II. The Worldwide Sounds: Rafi's Effect Past Lines

1. **Multifaceted Hug:**
   As we close our investigation, perceiving the worldwide music of Rafi's impact is fundamental. His voice, established in the dirt of Indian film, has navigated

social limits and resounded with crowds around the world. The all inclusiveness of feelings passed on through his tunes has worked with a culturally diverse hug, making Rafi an irreplaceable asset as well as a worldwide melodic symbol.

2. **Coordinated efforts and Social Trades:**

Rafi's coordinated efforts with global specialists stand as reference points of social trade. Whether it's the combination of his voice with Western melodic components or coordinated efforts with specialists from various areas of the planet, these occasions highlight the widespread language of music that Rafi talked. As we close our investigation, we perceive that Rafi's effect reaches out a long ways past the shores of his country, adding to a worldwide embroidery of melodic variety.

III. Instructive Importance: Rafi's Voice as an Educational Device

1. **Creative Instructional method:**
   As we make our determinations, it is essential to recognize the instructive importance implanted in Rafi's voice. His versions become more than simple melodic notes; they act as an instructive device, offering experiences into the subtleties of playback singing, vocal method, and the social setting of Indian music. Rafi's heritage reaches out past close to home reverberation to turn into a storehouse of creative teaching method.
2. **Sustaining Melodic Legacy:**

Instructive drives that perceive the significance of saving Rafi's melodic legacy add to the propagation of Indian melodic customs. The immortal nature of his voice guarantees its significance in scholarly educational plans, furnishing people in the future with a window into the rich embroidery of Indian playback singing.

IV. The Test of Conservation: Exploring Copyrights and Commercialization

1. **Copyright Difficulties:**
   Closing our investigation likewise involves standing up to the difficulties that encompass the safeguarding of Rafi's melodic inheritance. Copyright issues, lawful intricacies, and the sensitive harmony between business interests and social conservation are basic contemplations. As we recognize the difficulties, we should look for manageable arrangements that honor the validness of Rafi's effect on the universe of music.
2. **Moral Commercialization:**

Commercialization, while inescapable, requires moral contemplations. Finding some kind of harmony between giving recognition to Rafi's heritage and business practicality is a tightrope walk. As we finish up, it is basic to consider the obligation of safeguarding the certified pith of Rafi's commitments in the midst of the business tries that try to benefit from his getting through ubiquity.

V. Rafi's Persevering through Allure: A Finish of Flexibility and Emotive Profundity

1. **Adaptability Across Sorts:**
   Rafi's getting through advance lies in his unrivaled flexibility. From soul-mixing numbers that pull at the heartstrings to foot-tapping songs of devotion that imbue bliss, his voice easily crosses different types. The capacity to adjust to the changing melodic scene guarantees that Rafi's allure stays evergreen, closing every period with a commitment of coherence.

2. **Emotive Profundity and Human Association:**

At the core of Rafi's persevering through request is the emotive profundity that pervades his versions. His voice turns into a course for human feelings — love, happiness, distress, and reflection. As we close our process through Rafi's collection, we perceive that the persevering through association he produces with audience members is established in the legitimacy and genuineness of his emotive articulations.

VI. Rafi's Inheritance as a Social Embroidery: Commitments to Mid-twentieth Century India

1. **Social Symbol:**
   Rafi's inheritance isn't just a melodic peculiarity; a social embroidery mirrors the ethos of mid-twentieth century India. His melodies typify the fantasies, yearnings, and sentiment of a time set apart by friendly and social changes. As we finish up, we recognize Rafi as a playback vocalist as well as a social symbol whose voice resounds with the aggregate recollections of an age.

2. **Generational Handover:**

The giving over of Rafi's heritage starting with one age then onto the next turns into a critical topic in our decision. The tunes that were the soundtrack of one time track down new life in the encounters of succeeding ages. This generational handover is a demonstration of the immortality of Rafi's voice and its capacity to rise above the hindrances of existence.

VII. Rafi in the Computerized Age: Sustaining a Sonic Narrative

1. **Computerized Resurgence:**
   The advanced age reinvigorates Rafi's songs. Streaming stages, online networks, and computerized innovations work with a resurgence of his music, acquainting it with a worldwide crowd. The end includes perceiving the job of the advanced

scene in sustaining Rafi's sonic annal and guaranteeing that his voice keeps on resounding in the virtual spaces of the 21st 100 years.

2. **Remix Culture: A Challenged Inheritance:**

As we finish up, we wrestle with the intricacies of the remix culture that crosses with Rafi's inheritance. The computerized age delivers reevaluations, remixes, and discussions encompassing the conservation of creative honesty. Exploring this challenged scene turns into an essential piece of finishing up our investigation of Rafi's presence in the computerized domain.

VIII. End to the Gathering Collection: A Never-ending Recognition

1. **Thinking about the Collection's Job:**
   In the closing notes, we ponder the aggregation collection devoted to Mohammad Rafi's brilliant hits. This collection, as an organized excursion through Rafi's collection, embodies the diverse idea of his imaginativeness. It isn't just an assortment of tunes however a story that gives proper respect to the different elements of Rafi's voice, adding to the never-ending recognition that is his melodic heritage.

2. **Inheritance Past Limits:**

The collection turns into a microcosm of Rafi's inheritance past limits. It repeats around the world, reverberating with audience members who may not appreciate the language yet interface with the all inclusive feelings passed on through his voice. The end to the collection mirrors the global meaning of Rafi's getting through melodic splendor.

IX. The Enduring Effect: Rafi's Voice as a Narrator of Human Feelings

1. **A Narrator's Heritage:**
   As we draw the last notes of our investigation, we perceive Rafi as a playback vocalist as well as a narrator. His voice turns into the storyteller of stories loaded up with adoration, satisfaction, awfulness, and reflection. Finishing up our process includes recognizing Rafi's heritage as a narrator whose stories keep on enrapturing the hearts of millions.

2. **Reflecting Human Encounters:**

Rafi's voice, with its emotive reach and adaptability, mirrors the ups and downs of human encounters. In the end, we value the effect of his voice in catching the subtleties of life — its fantasies, sentiment, and feelings. Rafi's inheritance turns into a mirror to the human condition, a timeless impression of the horde feelings that characterize our reality.

X. The Unfading Reverberation: Rafi's Voice as an Undying Presence

1. **Rafi's Persevering through Everlasting status:**
   The end to our investigation envelops the persevering through everlasting status of Rafi's voice. It rises above the fleeting limitations, turning into an everlasting tune that reverberates through the ages. Rafi's voice isn't a remnant of the past however an undying presence that keeps on motivating, console, and interface with the human spirit.
2. **Inheritance as a Never-ending Accolade:**

In the last stanzas of our investigation, we recognize that the end isn't an endpoint yet an acknowledgment of Rafi's heritage as a never-ending recognition. The songs he created, the feelings he conveyed, and the effect he left on the universe of music stand as persevering through demonstrations of the immortal force of imaginative splendor.

A Challenge to Drench in the Brilliant Age

As we finish up this musical investigation of Mohammad Rafi's melodic odyssey, the end notes become a greeting. A greeting for audience members, old and new, to submerge themselves in the brilliant time of Indian film, to cross the domains of affection, satisfaction, and reflection through the songs of a maestro. Mohammad Rafi's voice, with its persevering through claim and immortal reverberation, stretches out a never-ending greeting to set out on an excursion through the tunes that reverberation across the ages — an excursion that rises above time and turns into a festival of the unfading tradition of one of India's most prominent playback vocalists.

6.1 Recap of the significance of "Voice of an Era: Mohammad Rafi's Golden Hits"

As we explore the melodic scene of "Voice of a Time: Mohammad Rafi's Brilliant Hits," a review venture becomes basic — an investigation into the significant importance that typifies this gathering collection. Past a simple assortment of melodies, this collection fills in as a sonic time case, protecting the quintessence of Mohammad Rafi's distinguished lifetime. In this recap, we dig into the complex layers that add to the collection's getting through influence, pondering its social, personal, and authentic importance.

1. **The Specialty of Curation: Creating an Immortal Story**
1. **Ordered Embroidered artwork:**
   At the core of the collection's importance lies the fastidious curation that winds around an ordered embroidery of Rafi's vocation. The excursion unfurls naturally, permitting audience members to navigate the advancement of his creativity from the early hits to the nostalgic jewels.
   The ordered game plan turns out to be more than a sequencing of tunes; a story reflects the excursion of a playback maestro through the records of Hindi film.

2. Topical Amicability:

The collection likewise embraces topical agreement, gathering tunes in view of feelings, temperaments, or types. This topical methodology rises above fleeting limits, making a durable story that enhances the close to home reverberation of Rafi's voice. Whether investigating heartfelt songs, euphoric hymns, or philosophical insights, the collection turns into an organized investigation of Rafi's flexibility.

II. Reverberations of Sentiment: Rafi's Captivation of the Heart

1. Soul-Mixing Ditties:

A huge element of the collection's reverberation is found in the reverberations of sentiment that Rafi's voice summons. Tunes like "Chaudhvin Ka Chand Ho" and "Tum Jo Mil Gaye Ho" become more than melodic arrangements; they are personal scenes where Rafi's voice catches the subtleties of affection, yearning, and despair. The collection, through these spirit blending numbers, turns into a demonstration of Rafi's capacity to express the most significant of human feelings.

2. Festivity of Affection:

Past the melancholic notes of sentiment, the collection envelops the festival of affection in melodies like "Aaj Mausam Bada Beimaan Hai" and "Yeh Jo Chilman Hai." Rafi's voice turns into a channel for glad articulations, imbuing these songs of devotion with an extravagance that reverberates with the celebratory soul of adoration. The collection, in its investigation of sentiment, typifies the immortal nature of Rafi's voice in summoning the horde aspects of adoration.

III. Exploring Many years: A Time-Travel Through Rafi's Collection

1. Early Hits:

The collection's importance is unpredictably connected to its investigation of Rafi's initial hits. Melodies like "Suhaani Raat Dhal Chuki" and "Jiya O Jiya Kuchh Bol Do" transport audience members to the incipient phases of Rafi's vocation, giving a brief look into the early stages that established the groundwork for his later brightness. The sequential excursion through these early hits turns into a nostalgic outing, interfacing the audience with the foundations of Rafi's melodic heritage.

2. Nostalgic Jewels:

As the collection advances, it wanders into the domain of nostalgic jewels that characterize the brilliant time of Hindi film. Every tune turns into a brushstroke on the material of an era long since past, mirroring the social subtleties, cultural desires, and realistic feel of mid-twentieth century India. The collection, in its route through many years, turns into a time-travel experience that rises above the limits of years and submerges the audience in the wistfulness of a period long past.

IV. Flexibility Released: The Collection's Exhibit of Rafi's Creative Reach

1. **Classes Investigated:**
   A recap of the collection's importance requires an investigation of Rafi's flexibility, which remains as a foundation of his melodic inheritance. The aggregation digs into assorted types, from old style versions like "Madhuban Mein Radhika" to the foot-tapping rhythms of "Yippee! Chahe Koi Mujhe Junglee Kahe." The collection turns into a grandstand of Rafi's creative reach, representing his capacity to consistently adjust to a bunch of melodic articulations.

2. **Close to home Reverberation:**

The flexibility isn't just an exhibit of specialized ability yet an epitome of close to home reverberation. Rafi's voice turns into an instrument of emotive narrating, whether conveying the philosophical thoughts in "Principal Zindagi Ka Saath Nibhata Chala Gaya" or the lively extravagance in "Badan Pe Sitare Lapete Huye." The collection, in its investigation of flexibility, underlines Rafi's significant effect in summoning a range of human feelings.

V. Coordinated efforts with Maestros: Rafi's Orchestra with Music Chiefs

1. **Notable Joint efforts:**
   The collection's importance stretches out to its festival of Rafi's joint efforts with amazing music chiefs. Each track turns into a demonstration of the ensemble made when Rafi's voice meets the organizations of maestros like S.D. Burman, Shankar-Jaikishan, and R.D. Burman. The cooperative sorcery unfurls in tunes like "Yeh Jo Mohabbat Hai" and "Yeh Jo Chilman Hai," where Rafi's voice turns into the highlight of ageless manifestations.

2. **Versatility Across Sounds:**

Past individual hits, the collection stresses Rafi's versatility across the soundscape created by various music chiefs. Whether exploring the traditional complexities of S.D. Burman's creations or embracing the exploratory hints of R.D. Burman, Rafi's voice consistently incorporates into different melodic scenes.

The collection turns into a demonstration of the harmonious connection between Rafi's voice and the virtuoso of notable music chiefs.

VI. The Worldwide Reverberation: Rafi's Voice Past Topographical Limits

1. **Multifaceted Hug:**
   One of the collection's significant aspects is its acknowledgment of Rafi's

worldwide reverberation. His voice rises above topographical limits, resounding with audience members around the world. Melodies like "Jeene Ke Hain Chaar Racket" become worldwide hymns, mirroring the widespread feelings implanted in Rafi's voice. The collection, in its affirmation of worldwide hug, positions Rafi as a social diplomat whose tunes resound with the human experience regardless of ethnicity.

2. **Coordinated efforts Past Lines:**

The importance stretches out to Rafi's joint efforts with worldwide specialists, adding to the collection's worldwide story. Cases where Rafi's voice amicably converges with assorted melodic customs become social crossing points that rise above borders. The collection turns into a demonstration of the worldwide effect of Rafi's voice and its capacity to cultivate multifaceted associations through the language of music.

VII. Computerized Resurgence: The Collection's Propagation in the Advanced Scene

1. **Availability Through Innovation:**
   In the computerized age, the collection acquires further importance as an impetus for Rafi's propagation in the advanced scene. Streaming stages, online networks, and computerized innovations guarantee the openness of his immortal tunes to a worldwide crowd. The collection turns into a vehicle for acquainting Rafi's brilliant hits with new audience members, propagating his heritage in the virtual spaces of the 21st hundred years.

2. **Difficulties of Remix Culture:**

The recap recognizes the difficulties presented by the remix culture and reevaluations of Rafi's works of art. Exploring the sensitive harmony between safeguarding the legitimacy of the first pieces and embracing the elements of the computerized period turns into a basic part of the collection's importance. It brings up issues about imaginative honesty and the moral contemplations encompassing remixes with regards to saving a melodic heritage.

VIII. Instructive Importance: The Collection as a Vault of Creative Teaching method

1. **Gaining from Rafi's Versions:**
   A recap includes perceiving the collection's instructive importance as a vault of imaginative teaching method. Each track turns into an illustration in playback singing, vocal procedure, and the social subtleties implanted in Rafi's versions. The collection remains as an asset for trying vocalists, music lovers, and researchers, adding to the propagation of Indian melodic practices.

2. **Safeguarding Social Legacy:**

Instructive drives that use the collection as a learning device assume a vital part in saving social legacy. By analyzing Rafi's versions, understudies gain experiences into the authentic and social settings of mid-twentieth century India. The collection, as a vessel for protecting social legacy, guarantees that Rafi's commitments stay significant across ages.

IX. Business Achievement and Moral Contemplations: Adjusting the Heritage

1. **Business Feasibility:**
   As we recap the collection's importance, we stand up to the double idea of business achievement and moral contemplations. The collection's fame and business suitability are innate parts of its prosperity, however finding some kind of harmony becomes critical. The recap prompts reflections on how business attempts meet with the obligation of safeguarding the authentic quintessence of Rafi's heritage.

2. **Moral Commercialization:**

Protecting the imaginative trustworthiness of Rafi's commitments in the midst of business attempts requires moral contemplations. The fragile harmony between business achievement and social safeguarding turns into a nuanced investigation. The recap brings issues to light about the difficulties and obligations related with guaranteeing that Rafi's inheritance isn't diminished to simple wares.

The Collection as an Immortal Recognition for Rafi's Inheritance

1. **Never-ending Recognition:**
   In finishing up our recap, that's what we confirm "Voice of a Time: Mohammad Rafi's Brilliant Hits" is in excess of a gathering; it is a never-ending recognition for Rafi's heritage. The collection's importance reaches out past a simple assortment of tunes, turning into a demonstration of the getting through force of Rafi's voice in molding the melodic scene of mid-twentieth century India.

2. **Greeting to Inundate:**

As the collection welcomes audience members to submerge themselves in the brilliant time of Indian film, the recap fills in as a sign of the extravagance implanted in Rafi's tunes. It is a challenge to navigate the profound scenes, social subtleties, and ageless articulations that characterize Rafi's commitment to the universe of music.

A Symphonious Reverberation That Perseveres

In these last notes, we recognize the consonant reverberation that perseveres through "Voice of a Period: Mohammad Rafi's Brilliant Hits." The collection, with its cautiously organized story, topical investigation, and affirmation of Rafi's worldwide effect, turns into an ensemble that rises above time. It remains as a demonstration of the persevering through tradition of a playback maestro whose voice keeps on reverberating through the ages — a reverberation that resounds with social, close to home, and verifiable importance. As the last notes wait, the collection turns out to be in excess of a melodic gathering; a festival of an immortal voice will be for all time carved in the aggregate memory of music fans and admirers of the brilliant period of Indian film.

6.2 Invitation for both Rafi enthusiasts and newcomers to experience the musical journey.

In the immense embroidery of Indian playback singing, the name Mohammad Rafi remains as an illuminator, a maestro whose voice rises above worldly limits, reverberating through the passages of time. As we stretch out this solicitation to both Rafi fans and novices the same, we leave on a melodic dream — an excursion that navigates the ups and downs of human feelings, investigates the social embroidery of mid-twentieth century India, and reveals the flexible masterfulness of a playback legend.

1. **Setting the Stage: Rafi's Persevering through Inheritance**
1. **The Eternal Voice:**
   At the center of this greeting lies the eternal voice of Mohammad Rafi. For devotees very much familiar with the subtleties of his versions, it is an amazing chance to return to the ageless songs that have turned into the soundtrack of ages. For rookies, a prologue to a voice has made a permanent imprint on the historical backdrop of Indian music — a challenge to find the extravagance, profundity, and general allure implanted in Rafi's vocal creativity.
2. **A Social Symbol:**

Rafi isn't only a playback vocalist; he is a social symbol whose commitments reach out past the domain of music. His melodies exemplify the fantasies, yearnings, and opinions of mid-twentieth century India, offering a window into the social and social ethos of the time. As we broaden this greeting, it is an affirmation of Rafi's job as a caretaker of social legacy and a storyteller of the aggregate encounters of a past time.

II. Exploring the Brilliant Hits: An Organized Excursion Through Time

1. **Topical Investigation:**
   This greeting unfurls as an organized excursion through Rafi's brilliant hits, every tune a diamond in the tremendous collection of his melodic heritage. The topical investigation welcomes devotees to rediscover recognizable songs while offering rookies an organized prologue to the diverse idea of Rafi's imaginativeness. From soul-blending songs to blissful hymns, the organized excursion is a demonstration of the flexibility that characterizes Rafi's voice.
2. **Ordered Embroidery:**

The ordered game plan of the brilliant hits fills in as a story string that winds through the various periods of Rafi's vocation. For fans, it is a nostalgic outing through a world of fond memories, an opportunity to remember the wizardry of every time. For rookies, it turns into a verifiable investigation, following the development of Rafi's style, articulation, and effect on the true to life and melodic scene of India.

III. Heartfelt Songs: Catching the Subtleties of Adoration

1. **Soul-Blending Anthems:**
   The greeting reaches out to the domain of sentiment, where Rafi's voice turns into the epitome of adoration's horde conceals. Fans will wind up submerged in the spirit mixing numbers that have characterized the heartfelt ethos of Hindi film. For newbies, it is a prologue to the unmatched capacity of Rafi to catch the subtleties of adoration, from the delicate to the enthusiastic, in melodies like "Chaudhvin Ka Chand Ho" and "Tum Jo Mil Gaye Ho."

2. **Festivity of Adoration:**

Past the melancholic notes, the excursion welcomes the two aficionados and newbies to delight in the festival of affection. Playful songs of praise like "Aaj Mausam Bada Beimaan Hai" and "Yeh Jo Chilman Hai" grandstand Rafi's capacity to mix euphoria and abundance into his versions. The greeting is an affirmation that Rafi's voice isn't restricted to a solitary profound register however ranges the whole range of human experience.

IV. Nostalgic Pearls: Navigating the Past Times

1. **Early Hits: A Brief look into Rafi's Beginnings:**
   As we stretch out the challenge to investigate Rafi's initial hits, fans are moved to the incipient phases of his vocation. Melodies like "Suhaani Raat Dhal Chuki" and "Jiya O Jiya Kuchh Bol Do" become entryways to the early stages that established the groundwork for the maestro's later brightness. For rookies, this section of the excursion is a verifiable undertaking, uncovering the foundations of a melodic inheritance.

2. **Exploring the Brilliant Period:**

The greeting proceeds with venture through the nostalgic jewels characterize the brilliant time of Hindi film. Every tune turns into a brushstroke on the material of an era long since past, mirroring the social subtleties, cultural goals, and realistic style of mid-twentieth century India. The greeting is a vivid encounter, permitting the two lovers and rookies to navigate the domains of wistfulness and social legacy.

V. Grandstand of Adaptability: Rafi's Imaginative Reach Released

1. **Kinds Investigated:**
   Rafi's flexibility remains as a reference point all through this greeting, welcoming both prepared fans and novices to observe the broadness of his creative reach. The excursion crosses different sorts, from traditional interpretations like "Madhuban Mein Radhika" to the foot-tapping rhythms of "Hurray! Chahe Koi Mujhe Junglee Kahe." Fans will delight in the recognizable brightness, while newbies will find the vivid idea of Rafi's collection.

2. **Profound Reverberation:**

Flexibility, for Rafi's situation, is definitely not a simple presentation of specialized ability however an encapsulation of close to home reverberation. This fragment of the excursion investigates how Rafi's voice turns into an instrument of emotive narrating. Whether conveying philosophical thoughts in "Principal Zindagi Ka Saath Nibhata Chala Gaya" or radiating energetic abundance in "Badan Pe Sitare Lapete Huye," Rafi's close to home profundity welcomes audience members to associate with the range of human feelings.

VI. Coordinated efforts with Maestros: An Orchestra of Melodic Virtuoso

1. **Notable Joint efforts:**
   The greeting stretches out to the cooperative wizardry woven between Rafi's voice and the virtuoso of unbelievable music chiefs. Each track turns into a demonstration of the orchestra made when Rafi works together with maestros like S.D. Burman, Shankar-Jaikishan, and R.D. Burman.
   Devotees will rediscover the subtleties of these famous organizations, while novices will observer the consistent joining of Rafi's voice into different melodic scenes.

2. **Melodic Flexibility:**

The cooperative excursion likewise accentuates Rafi's flexibility across sounds made by various music chiefs. Whether exploring the traditional complexities of S.D. Burman's creations or embracing the exploratory hints of R.D. Burman, Rafi's voice flawlessly incorporates into changed melodic conditions. The greeting turns into an investigation of the cooperative connection between Rafi's voice and the unmatched virtuoso of notorious music chiefs.

VII. Worldwide Reverberation: Rafi's Voice Past Topographical Limits

1. **Culturally diverse Hug:**
   The greeting rises above topographical lines, perceiving Rafi's worldwide reverberation. His voice, established in the dirt of Indian film, resounds with crowds around the world. Melodies like "Jeene Ke Hain Chaar Clamor" become worldwide hymns, mirroring the widespread feelings implanted in Rafi's voice. The

greeting is an affirmation that Rafi's songs are not restricted to a solitary culture yet have turned into a common melodic language that rises above ethnicities.

2. **Joint efforts Past Boundaries:**

This portion of the excursion investigates Rafi's coordinated efforts with world-wide craftsmen, making social convergences that encourage culturally diverse associations. The greeting turns into a tribute to the worldwide effect of Rafi's voice and its capacity to connect social holes through the widespread language of music. Devotees and newbies the same are welcome to observe the broad impact of Rafi's tunes past the limits of geological limits.

VIII. Computerized Resurgence: A Sonic Odyssey in the Virtual Domain

1. **Openness Through Innovation:**
   In the computerized age, the greeting takes on another aspect as Rafi's songs experience a resurgence in the virtual domain. Streaming stages, online networks, and computerized innovations guarantee the openness of his immortal hits to a worldwide crowd. The greeting turns into an investigation of the manners by which innovation has propagated Rafi's heritage, making his songs open to another age of audience members.

2. **Difficulties of Remix Culture:**

As the excursion unfurls in the computerized scene, the greeting defies the intricacies of the remix culture. Rafi's works of art face reevaluations and remixes, starting discussions about protecting the credibility of the first creations. Devotees and novices the same are welcome to explore the difficulties presented by the remix culture, pondering the moral contemplations encompassing the reevaluation of ageless melodic show-stoppers.

IX. Instructive Importance: A Learning Undertaking through Rafi's Interpretations

1. **Gaining from the Maestro:**
   The greeting stretches out to the instructive importance implanted in Rafi's versions. Each track turns into an illustration in playback singing, vocal method, and the social subtleties unpredictably woven into Rafi's creativity. Devotees and newbies are welcome to dive into the subtleties of Indian music, investigating the specialized brightness and emotive profundity that characterize Rafi's commitments to the universe of playback singing.

2. **Saving Social Legacy:**

Instructive drives that use the greeting as a learning device assume a significant part in protecting social legacy. By taking apart Rafi's interpretations, understudies gain bits of knowledge into the verifiable and social settings of mid-twentieth century India. The greeting turns into a call to teachers, researchers, and lovers to perceive the collection as a significant asset for propagating the rich embroidery of Indian melodic customs.

Consonant Reverberation in the Hearts of Audience members

1. **A Never-ending Accolade:**
   As the greeting approaches its decision, it turns into a never-ending accolade for the tradition of Mohammad Rafi. The tunes created by Rafi, exhibited in this excursion, stand as ageless demonstrations of the getting through force of imaginative brightness. The greeting isn't simply an investigation yet a festival of a voice that rises above time, making a permanent imprint on the hearts of fans and rookies the same.

2. **A Continuous Orchestra:**

The finishing up notes of the greeting reverberation with the comprehension that Rafi's songs are not restricted to a particular period or age. They are essential for a continuous orchestra, reverberating through time and welcoming audience members to participate in the agreeable festival of one of India's most noteworthy playback artists. Lovers and rookies are welcome to become basic members in this ensemble, guaranteeing that Rafi's voice keeps on resounding through the ages.

An Immortal Festival of Rafi's Melodic Odyssey

As we close this invitational journey into Mohammad Rafi's melodic odyssey, the last harmonies wait as a demonstration of the persevering through reverberation of his voice. The greeting, stretched out to both prepared fans and inquisitive novices, turns into a festival of songs as well as a festival of the common human experience that Rafi's voice embodies. In the last harmonies, we track down an immortal festival — an affirmation that Rafi's songs will keep on being treasured, embraced, and passed on as a valuable heritage in the stupendous ensemble of Indian music.

www.ingramcontent.com/pod-product-compliance
Lightning Source LLC
LaVergne TN
LVHW020921200726
843506LV00011B/1755